MAKING PEACE
WITH YOUR WORK

MAKING
PEACE
WITH YOUR WORK

An Invitation to Find Meaning in the Madness

Delorese Ambrose, Ed.D.

Expert Publishing, Inc.
Andover, Minnesota

"My Soul Seeks Stopping" used with permission by Wendy von Oech *Stages of Personal Power* model and description adapted with permission from Janet O. Hagberg

ISBN 10: 1-931945-38-1
ISBN 13: 978-1-931945-38-7

Library of Congress Catalog Number: 2006924010

Printed in the United States

First Printing: April 2006

10 09 08 07 06   6 5 4 3 2 1

Expert Publishing, Inc.
14314 Thrush Street NW
Andover, MN 55304-3330
1-877-755-4966
www.expertpublishinginc.com

Dedication

To my mother, Rose,
who taught me the joy of work
and
my grandchildren,
Olivia Rose and Grant Christopher,
whose work awaits them.

Work is love made visible.
And if you cannot work with love but only
with distaste, it is better that you should
leave your work and sit at the gate of the
temple and take alms of those who work
with joy.

—THE PROPHET, KAHLIL GIBRAN

Table of Contents

Foreword

Making Peace with Your Work describes the inner journey involved in integrating our spirit—our soul—into our work life so we are not separated from who we truly are when we are at work. Delorese Ambrose offers practical ways for all of us to live undivided lives. Every chapter contains not only rich concepts but also examples of people who have put that idea into practice. She herself experienced a steady rise to success, after which she grappled with the loss of meaning in her work. That experience brought her to a more authentic way of living and working. She tells her story, and the stories of workers from various walks of life, and offers ideas that are inspiring and challenging.

Suzanne Anderson-Zahir, one of Ambrose's colleagues whose story is cited in the book, describes her own experience this way:

I have come to understand that I am Spirit. This understanding has allowed me to unite my life and my work as one. I now understand that my work takes place all the time, whether I'm with family or friends or in the organized workplace. It's simply Spirit calling me to be wherever I am. Wherever I show up is where I'm supposed to be working. I am now connected with Higher Purpose. When we make that connection there is less need to push. Wherever I show up Spirit has sent me there for a reason. Whatever clients show up or whatever situation presents itself, if I am invited in, I am the one who is supposed to be there for some reason. My work is to figure how best to be in that situation.

Frederick Buechner, in *Wishful Thinking*, says, "The place God calls you to is the place where your deep gladness and the world's deep hunger meet" (p. 95). Perhaps that is what gives Anderson-Zahir's work meaning and mystery. She works at the juncture where her deep gladness and the world's hunger meet, linking her heart's desires with right livelihood.

Ambrose teaches that if we stop to journey inward, we can connect with our present work in a more meaningful way and make choices going forward that lead to more satisfying personal and organizational results. *Making Peace with Your Work* is a wonderful example of her own efforts at listening to her "Inner Caller" and modeling the way. It joins her accumulated wisdom and experience with the wisdom and experience of workers everywhere throughout history.

She is at a point in her life where she must call the rest of us to make peace with our work. I am grateful to her for the invitation. *Making Peace* challenges me to listen more consistently for guidance and to ask for the courage to live out what I hear.

–Janet O. Hagberg, author of *Real Power,* social activist, healer

Acknowledgments

Deepak Chopra reminds us that "Whenever we try to pick out anything by itself, we find it hitched to everything else in the universe." The writing of this book and the ideas in it are hitched to everyone whose work and whose ideas have touched my life. Let me mention just a few.

In many ways this book is an offspring of the Real Power Network to whom I am deeply grateful. Special thanks to my friend and mentor Janet Hagberg for your insights into real power, and to Network members Donna Bennett, Janae Bower, Pat Casello, Fay Chobin, LaRee Ewers, Robin Getman, and Sharron Stockhausen, for your role as midwives, reviewers, interviewees, and cheerleaders.

Several of you opened your hearts and shared your personal stories: Suzanne Anderson-Zahir, Frances Baldwin, Donna Bennett, Jim Brown, Vincent Brown, Bob Chobin, Myrna and Timothy Bullock, Richard Friend, Robin Getman, Jerry McNellis, Sara Merz, Bruce Nolan, Betsy

Pickren, and Diana Whitney. Anyone who reads this book will be deeply touched, and changed in some special way, because of your generosity.

Special thanks to everyone at the Institute for Management Studies (IMS), a world class organization with whom I'm proud to work. You have long understood the importance of helping people and organizations make a difference by thinking differently.

Deep gratitude to my clients who make my work and my livelihood possible. By opening your doors and inviting me to challenge, teach, and to be a partner in your change efforts, you have added meaning to my life.

My colleagues in Atlanta's Organizational Change Alliance have been a constant source of inspiration, information, and friendship. Rob Johnson and Betsy Pickren gave generously of their time as reviewers and stimulated my thinking in numerous ways. K. T. Connor generously shared her insights about the "selves" we bring to work.

Of course, this book would not be in your hands without the patient, impeccable work of Harry Stockhausen at Expert Publishing, Inc. and the design genius of Tom Heller who so beautifully captured the essence of this work.

Most of all, I am deeply grateful to my family and friends for your unstinting support, your patience, your kindness, and your belief in me. As I composed this book, you tolerated my disappearing acts and my rambling on about ideas forming in my head as you very lovingly encouraged me to hang in with the project no matter what. Special thanks to my daughter-in-law, Lillian, for the many ways you nurture family. Yours is the most important work of all.

Introduction

A colleague of mine recently congratulated a relative on his retirement. With sad eyes the new retiree muttered, "Forty years in the same job, and I hated every moment of it." I couldn't shake his comment from my thoughts. Was it possible for this poor soul to have found some meaning, some sense of community, and some satisfaction in serving his industry for the better part of his life? How did he come to feel he had no other recourse? Surely, he'd had some high points in his years of hard work. Why, in the end, did he define his work experiences by the low points?

> "Man's search for meaning is the primary motivation in his life."
>
> —VICTOR FRANKL

Thankfully, most people do not share this man's experience. But his story quickened my determination to finish this book. Let's face it, it's unrealistic to expect that our work will always be fulfilling. There are grueling aspects of any occupation, and our personal preference, values, and needs sometimes clash with those of our work places. My neighbor Kathy enjoys her work as a marketing representative. She loves being out and about in the field, but dreads being bogged down in the office.

We don't always have control over such challenges. There may be times when the compensation we receive doesn't quite measure up to the time and effort we put in, or where competing priorities and meeting mania snuff out our creativity and sap our energy.

If you work in the emergency room of a hospital, stress goes with the territory. If you are in charge of an organization, or are forced to work long hours for any reason, you might find that your work competes with your family for your time.

What concerns me, and what this book addresses, is how we make meaning in the madness. Some people simply go through their work on autopilot day in, day out from paycheck to paycheck—it's "just a job." Some see work as a necessary burden of adult life. Even the most satisfied among us face aspects of their work that need healing.

More troubling, there is evidence that increasingly these days, we find ourselves at war with work. If we are spending the prime years of our adult life and our best waking hours wedded to work, we'd better make sure we find a way to make peace with it.

So how well does your work, work for you? Have you managed to create work that is stimulating, profitable, and satisfying most of the time? Do you greet your workday with gratitude and hope, or do you cringe at the thought of what's ahead? Maybe you landed your dream job. Are you waking up to find it's a living nightmare, or is it more than you dreamed possible? Chances are your work puts food on the table. Does it also feed your soul? If you pride yourself on working hard to make a living, does your work leave enough room for your living?

Perhaps you've been in the workplace for a while, and have enjoyed many successes. Do you find yourself wondering what's next? Most likely you work, or have worked, for an organization that has a vision and mission that gives it direction. What is the vision and mission that guides your work and your life? How compatible are your personal values and priorities with those of your organization?

I pose these questions because my work is about work. My career puts me in touch with people worldwide who seek the best that work—and life—has to offer. When people attend my seminars, seek me out as a coach, or invite me into their workplaces as a consultant, they are thinking about change. They show up in a variety of ways. Some don't quite know where to start or where exactly they're headed. Others are clear and need support as they make transition. Many are stuck.

Overworked clients tell me they are spinning their wheels like trapped gerbils trying to get better results faster and faster, with less and less time, and too few resources. They want to stop the insanity.

Employers tell me their employees expect them to be all-powerful and all knowing—or at least very smart and effective. But the rapids of change are so unrelenting, there isn't time to stop, reflect, strategize, and make smart moves. Not surprisingly, these executives log long hours. One half-jokingly says, "These days the only difference between my office and my home is the fact that one has a bed."

High achievers seek me out when they hit a wall. Many have accomplished everything they set out to do. Business is booming, their clients are satisfied, they love what they do, and their nest eggs have hatched more than they ever dreamed possible. But still they wonder: Is this all there is? They are searching for a more satisfying experience of work.

My client Ken is executive director of a non-profit organization. He is deeply committed to community renewal and has spent a lifetime as an activist, volunteer, and employee in social change agencies. Unfortunately, in his present position, which he has held for fifteen years, he is at odds with a board of directors he feels is out of touch with the nonprofit's mission and slow to change. This uneasy relationship is almost unbearable at times. He worries about the long-term impact on himself, his staff, and ultimately those he serves. Ken says, "I like my work, but I hate my job."

Gloria, an investment banker who just turned fifty, tells me she is suddenly seized with panic because, regrettably, after years of hard work, she still hasn't socked away enough for the future. "I might have to work forever!" she laments. Her colleague Jonathan, who works in the same office asks, "What's so bad about working forever?" Work is so central to his identity and gives his life so much meaning that the idea of retirement seems ludicrous to Jonathan. At mid-life his concerns are: "What will I work at next? How can I reinvent my work in the second half of my life?"

Sandra, comptroller for a rapidly growing engineering firm that has gone through a difficult, messy merger, attended a leadership retreat I conducted in Stone Mountain, Georgia. Burnt out and anxious, she was looking for an experience where she could stop and reflect on her life. Her six-figure salary, she told me, is both a blessing and a curse, because she feels that in today's job market, if she chooses to move on, or is forced out, it will be difficult to find an organization willing to match her salary. Sandra fantasizes daily about walking away from the job, perhaps even changing careers and settling for a lesser salary if necessary. But as a single parent, she faces the financial challenge of putting three teenagers through college. She is not likely to risk starting over at this stage. She lives with the stressful contradiction of secretly wanting to leave, yet still hoping she will not be a casualty of her company's difficult transition.

Denny, a division manager in a Fortune 500 company, is struggling with the personal trauma of shutting down a major facility that will put hundreds of loyal lifetime employees, including his best friend, out of work. Denny admits he feels guilty. He can hardly find words to describe what it feels like to implement a decision hatched at levels above him. He thinks about how families, including his own, will be affected since his wife and the wife of the friend he must fire, as well as both sets of children, were [formerly] all family friends. He questions his faith. He questions his ethics. He has decided he will himself take early retirement if the opportunity arises.

Like Ken, Gloria, Jonathan, and the others in my examples, we each have a story to tell about some aspect of our work that needs healing. My work for over twenty years has been to listen, learn, and help people rewrite the stories of their work to create more satisfying personal and organizational outcomes.

My goal in writing this book is to capture and share what I have learned so far. Throughout I will tell my story and the stories of workers from all walks of life who have successfully made peace with some aspect of their work, or who are in the process of discovering how to do so. Most of the stories are uplifting. They remind us of our inner power, our capacity to transcend adversity or to be conscious partners in our work experience. A few are cautionary tales that remind us of the suffering that comes when we are at war with our work.

Ironically, the idea for *Making Peace with Your Work* first presented itself at a personal low point where I found myself at war with my work. At the zenith of my career, I was overtaken with feelings of ambivalence about my life and about the work that resided at the center of it. It began with a subtle questioning of my choices and escalated into a full-blown crisis. I had built a successful consulting firm in Pittsburgh and was respected locally as a community volunteer. I was also an award-winning educator and organizational development consultant, privileged to serve on important boards, and on the graduate management faculty of a highly regarded university. I traveled internationally teaching and coaching employees—supporting them in their search for better ways to manage self, lead others, and get effective personal and organizational results.

Traditional definitions of success tell us we should work hard, take on increasing amounts of responsibility, earn, spend, and save as much as we can, and make a difference locally or globally. For years I scored high on these success criteria, but I didn't *feel* successful. Things looked great externally, but internally, I was living a lie. Frankly, my work had taken over my life.

The irony was that I continued to tell myself and the clients I coached that it is important to lead blended lives, to create time for both action and reflection, to do well, and to do good in serving others. I affirmed that work should incorporate creativity and fun. I taught in seminars that the best leaders were self-reflective and courageous enough to "bring their souls to work." I reminded people that if we make a good living, but our lives don't work, then we are not truly successful. I said these things, and I believed them. Yet I found it increasingly difficult to live these values. My awareness of this mushroomed into an inner crisis—a crisis of integrity, which I describe more fully in chapter nine.

In the end my upheaval was a gift, for it became a most important journey of personal discovery. I had come to a wall and the way through was to learn firsthand how to move from traditional definitions of success to a personal definition that would give my work and my life more significance.

I was a ready student, and the teachers appeared. They showed up as clients, trainees, and colleagues from all walks of life. Some were senior employees reflecting on the long history of their work lives and lessons learned in retrospect. Many were boomers like myself, driven to achieve, yet facing the uncertainties of mid-life as they pondered their next steps. Some were thirty-something-year-olds emerging into decision-making positions, or starry-eyed newcomers anxious to make their mark at work, but not yet knowing how.

I convened focus groups, led weekend retreats, and conducted interviews with supervisors and supervisees, physicians and bankers, nonprofit workers and business executives, military personnel and civilian government employees. I talked with human resources professionals, artists, entrepreneurs, and technicians and with people who had survived multiple downsizings and those charged with making decisions to execute such layoffs. I listened with renewed interest, and in a keener, more personal way, to what attendees in my seminars had to say about work.

I learned much about how the generations in our workplaces see their work. I listened as the thirty-something crowd reflected on their latch key experiences and their views of their work-obsessed boomer parents who were often downsized out of jobs through no fault of their own. I made note of the ambivalence of boomers who talked of their impending retirement with mixed feelings and who redefined retirement so it meant still more work—hopefully, more meaningful work—afterwards. I listened and took notes as close friends and colleagues alike described their passages through predictable work life quandaries. Most importantly I scheduled many hours daily, and occasional personal retreats, to give myself quiet time for reflection.

I learned, again, that once we *decide* to do our work in earnest, we do not go alone. As Joseph Campbell put it, "a thousand unseen hands appear" to help us.

In reaching out for help, I landed into a loving circle of like-minded colleagues—the Real Power Network—convened by Janet Hagberg to support those who teach and live the stages of personal power model described in chapter nine. Each member of the network was a high achiever. Each coincidentally was in the midst of a significant work/life transition. Each was about to step off a cliff into the unknown; the network provided a safety net below and helped us materialize wings for our flight. It was, without doubt, Divine synchronicity.

On my way to my first Real Power Network meeting, my friend Frances Baldwin with whom I had had many deep conversations about transforming our work, gifted me with a poem, titled "My Soul Seeks Stopping," which perfectly captured where we both were at the time. I read the poem to the network members by way of introduction. It was greeted with a collective sigh of recognition and a few teary eyes. I later phoned the author, Wendy Von Oech, to ask her permission to use the poem in this book. She was most surprised, she told me, to learn that the "little poem she wrote for herself" at a time of personal transition had found its way out into the world. In part, the poem reads:

> ...*I've come to the place call Stopping,*
> *where I must come to know*
> *the well within that has no end,*
> *that I take wherever I go.*
> *I take with me the darkness,*
> *the life-giving water, the unseen light.*
> *I take with me the vision*
> *of calm and still, of dark and bright.*
>
> *When I return to Going,*
> *to action, product, and goal,*
> *my heart will be strong, my mind awake*
> *and love and light will fill my soul.*
> *Now I can step with purpose,*
> *with guidance, direction, and grace,*
> *for I move with the wisdom of Stopping*
> *that time cannot erase.*

© 1991 WENDY VON OECH, *Used with permission.*

How The Book Works

My stopping and the earnest conversations during that period have given me some ideas about the meaning, the madness, and the mystery of work. I lay these ideas out, laced together with real-life accounts of others like yourself who are searching for ways to transcend the struggles and paradoxes of work, to find beauty and meaning in the madness.

As you read these accounts, you may become reacquainted with the wide-eyed new employee you once were, who entered the workplace hoping to do something significant, eager to experience the wonder and rewards of work. Or you may relate to the story of someone whose work is still deeply satisfying, but who is wondering how to go deeper, or move forward to the next phase of life and work. Along with these personal accounts, you will find ideas that can help you move to a new vantage point from which to renew your passion, connect with your purpose, or heed your "Inner Caller"—that quiet whisper within each of us that nudges us to re-examine or find the wisdom in our present situation.

Some of you may be facing the possibility of being displaced as your organization restructures. Others of you may find your work currently eclipses your life, and you want to regain your equilibrium. My hope is you will get new ideas for finding what's right in the midst of what's wrong. I do not pretend to offer right answers for everyone. I do invite you to look more deeply at the story you are composing in your relationship with work.

PART I: THE MEANING AND THE MYSTERY OF WORK examines work in all of its complexity: as an income-producing job and as a call to serve humanity; as growth-producing, life-enhancing fun and as backbreaking toil; as the thing that robs us of our leisure and the thing that "gives substance to life." We learn that, ultimately, we must come to see work as a two-faced companion that has the potential to heal or harm, depending on the stance we take in our relationship with it. Once we accept this paradox, making peace with our work becomes easier.

PART II: THE MADNESS: THREE QUESTIONS TO PONDER invites you to reflect on the madness of working in the war zones and the fast lanes at a time in our history where work is riddled with perpetual turmoil brought on by unprecedented change and uncertainty. The final question, "Do You Bring Your Inner Self To Work?" is the pivotal question on which this book turns. Organizational life unwittingly encourages us to leave our true selves behind when we enter our workplaces. When we do this, we lose perspective, purpose, passion, and creativity. So does our organization.

PART III: INNER WORK: THE PATH TO MAKING PEACE reminds us that our most important work is introspection—stopping to align our inner yearnings with our outer world. There is no need to be perpetually swept along by the madness of a work culture that is itself searching for meaning and making its own false starts in the process. Inner work, the process of stopping to reflect on ourselves, calls us to be mindful of the tempo and the rhythm of our work experience and pace ourselves so we can stop, reflect, and renew ourselves.

A centerpiece of this section is Janet Hagberg's brilliant model of the six stages of personal power in organizations. Described in detail in her book, *Real Power—Stages of Personal Power in Organizations,* this model teaches us to look beyond the limits of organizational achievement and success, to find "real power," the kind that comes from within.

PART IV: THE PEACE PACT invites you to renegotiate your terms of engagement with work. This begins with a willingness to make peace with our fears. Instead of waiting for things to change, for the boss to get it together, or for the economy to turn around, we can choose to learn from our work experience and transform it. And even if we're stuck, held hostage by a lack of skills, student loans, social biases, or life constraints, we can still *choose* to have a different experience of our stuckness—one that ultimately can be liberating if we are willing to confront ourselves, make peace with our fears, and risk being different.

If you are currently living out someone else's definition of success, this section of the book provides ideas on how you can re-examine your heart's desires, and redefine success so that it works for you. It challenges old assumptions about work (*who says you can't mix business with pleasure?*) and offers dozens of tips on ways to be more intentional about your relationship with work.

As you negotiate a peace pact with work, I hope you come to learn, in the words of Margaret Wheatley, that "there is a simpler way...a new way of being in the world without fear. Being in the world with play and creativity... Being willing to learn and to be surprised." This awareness will afford us a better chance of keeping our organizational commitment to excellence and creativity, efficiency and effectiveness. At the same time, it will help us to keep our personal commitment to making an honest living and living a life that works.

PART I

The Meaning
and
The Mystery of Work

ONE

How Work Works

To live is to work. So every day we wake up and go about our work, trading precious hours of our lives for whatever work offers or demands of us. We work as caregivers tending the home front, raising children, healing the sick, or assisting the needy. We work as problem-solvers, policy makers, manual laborers, or craftspeople creating goods and delivering services. Often we leave home, family, and a good measure of freedom behind to enter workplaces where we spend our best waking hours—and likely the best years of our adult lives—as employers and employees. In between work, we eek out time for leisure and personal relationships wherever we can: two weeks vacation here, a day off there, or for some, the coveted weekend where we play catch-up with the rest of our lives, while planning for the workweek ahead. Of course, if we are children, we do school work in preparation for adult work later on.

Clearly work is about more than earning pay. True, at the physical and material level, work feeds, clothes, and shelters us. But work extends beyond the basic need to survive. It also feeds our self-worth and gives our life meaning. Through work we stretch our minds, make a difference with our artistry, apply our technical skills to solving human problems, and discover ourselves as we push beyond seeming limits to serve, acquire, and innovate. Work goes beyond using talents, skills, or our minds and hands to complete tasks, solve problems, or meet goals. Work is fundamental to all human endeavors. To work is our nature. Perhaps the most apt example is found in the very bodies that make our work possible. We stay alive for as long as the system of organs in the human body work. When they cease to work we die.

DEFINING WORK

Throughout this book I use the word "work" in its broadest sense, to refer to whatever needs to be done, wherever it needs to be done, and by whomever. (I do, however, exclude the "work" of drug dealers and others whose activities cause harm, rather than offer help.) I use "work" to describe the job, career, or any activity performed in service to others, whether for extrinsic rewards like money or for intrinsic satisfaction. "Work" describes activities aimed at basic sustenance such as raising a family or altruistic ones such as volunteering to help those in need. "Work" also encompasses creative expression for whatever purpose: making music, crafting art, or pursuing a path of inner spiritual work.

When we meet the Bakers, the Cooks, the Farmers, or the Carpenters we are reminded that in many ways our work defines us. We introduce one acquaintance to another and quickly add, "Joan is a lawyer with the firm of Shoemaker, Brakeman, Farmer, and Freedman," or "Jim is a miner down in West Virginia." Or we meet someone new, and instinctively ask, "So what do you *do?*" Why do we describe people in terms of their livelihood? Why do we want to know their occupation? Perhaps it is because humans seek meaning, and like Albert Einstein, we believe that, "Work is the only thing that gives substance to life."

Work may define us. But trying to define work is tricky business. I can think of no word in our language more laden with contradictory meanings. I mention to a friend that I'm composing a book on *Making Peace with Your Work.* "Great!" she enthuses, "I can't wait to read it. My *job* is driving me nuts. Don't get me wrong. It's a good job that pays well, and I have no intention of leaving anytime soon, but it's the kind of *work* that's thankless."

"Hmm," I'm thinking. "Her *job* pays, but the *work* stinks."

Ken, the non-profit executive director in my earlier example, says, "I like my work, but I hate my job." I take it to mean he is linking *work* to higher purpose, and *job* to grueling activities such as implementing ill-advised board directives or dealing with tough work relationships.

In contrast to Ken, Elsie, a server in my favorite restaurant, sees work as potentially laborious. "Thankfully," she says, "my *job* doesn't feel like *work* because I love people and I kid around with my customers all day." In Elsie's mind, *work* is what happens when your *job* ceases to be fun.

Could it be that our ambivalence about work shows up in the complex and varied ways we conceptualize, experience, and talk about work? Consider these five examples pulled from a journal I kept for weeks in which I noted a dozen different ways I heard people use the word "work":

1. "He makes a good living as a steelworker." (Work as livelihood.)
2. "This works!" or "Let's work it out." (Work as problem-solving.)
3. "She works in stained glass." (Work as artistry.)
4. "Whew. This is work!" (Work as toil.)
5. "I'm pursuing my life's work," or "God's work is never done." (Work as vocation, calling, or spiritual practice.)

Let's take a closer look at these five manifestations of work.

WORK AS LIVELIHOOD

I'm not sure whether children are born this way or whether we school them as toddlers to start thinking about their work, but from the moment they learn to talk, they begin to self-identify with work they consider glamorous or meaningful in some way. "I want to be a firefighter." "I want to be a nurse." Or, as a five-year-old recently told me, "I want to be a manager, like my Daddy, and be the boss of all the people." When our youngsters declare their career aspirations, we perk up and listen, and perhaps gently steer them in the "right" direction—one that will guarantee a good (i.e., lucrative) living and perhaps social status as well. When his three-year-old declared, "I want to pack groceries for everyone at the supermarket when I grow up," my friend nervously corrected him in that fatherly voice that says let me teach you the right way. "No, son. You're going to MIT so you can be an engineer."

Finding work that allows us to make a *good living* has always been both the preoccupation and occupation of adult life. As hunters and gatherers we braved the wilds and wrestled with nature, taxing our minds and bodies to solve the problem of survival. With the agricultural age, we forged new solutions to this age-old problem. We shifted from hunting and gathering to farming and harvesting. To create a more stable, less taxing existence, we cultivated the land and bred animals. Through droughts and times of plenty, poor crops and good ones, we persisted in our work, wrestling with dilemmas and resolving difficulties. As we migrated from field to factory, our strategy shifted from producing to consuming. We "progressed" from growing food to buying it. We left the communal life where work emanated from home for factory jobs where we manned and mimicked machines as women took over the domain of the home and family life. We waged war with work as long hours and grueling routines put work life at odds with home life, creating the cultural blueprint for today's workplaces.

WORK AS PROBLEM-SOLVING

Humans are natural problem-solvers. This is a good thing, because at the heart of survival lies the ability to resolve difficulties and get the right outcomes. How do we get crops to grow in a harsh geographic environment? How do we get a thing to work? How do we heal the sick, teach a child, please a customer, feed our families? How do we transform a challenging situation into a more tenable one? In answering such questions, we have used our problem-solving prowess to innovate beyond what not long ago was thought to be humanly impossible.

> "Nothing will work unless you do."
>
> —MAYA ANGELOU

The exciting moments at work come when we set about finding solutions to the quandaries of living. "Wasn't that great!" the elevator repairman in my building gushes to his assistant, as I walk past them in the hallway. "I love it when we solve the tough ones like this one."

At work, problem-solvers show up with many different orientations, which I describe in my earlier book, *Healing The Downsized Organization*. Some are specialists who hone their craft or deploy their talents in a specific field or occupation. Some are directors who lead, manage, or supervise people and projects to get the best results. Others are thrill-seekers driven to live on the edge or to do the thing that has never been done before. The joy in their work comes solving the unsolvable. Mavericks and entrepreneurs are another breed of problem-solvers. What gets them juiced up is challenging the status quo to explore new ways of solving problems or striking out on their own to create the business or the work that fuels their independence. Caretakers show up in a wide range of occupations that address the problems associated with healing, protecting, defending, and supporting others.

At the twenty-first century, we are being called again to transform our work and workplaces in a deeper, more satisfying way. Jobs, the discrete artificial units into which we have traditionally divided up the work of our organizations, were created to facilitate division of labor as we synchronized, standardized, and mass produced goods and services to sustain ourselves. Along with jobs, hierarchies, turfs, and silos all became important features of organizational life in every sector. This design worked well during the Industrial Era. Now the boundaries defined by jobs are getting fuzzy.

Today, we face new problems, many of which have been created by our successes at solving former problems. Now, what needs to be done and who is available to do it changes so rapidly that we must again redefine how we work. Besides, in our search for meaning, we too are changing. We now seek interdependence over autocracy. We are breaking down hierarchies to make room for cross-functional work teams. We are forming new alliances, cross-training workers, merging with former competitors, outsourcing jobs, hiring contingency workers, and making other dramatic moves to shore up resources for economic viability in uncertain times. In short, the problem we now face is how to reinvent work so it continues to work for us.

WORK AS ARTISTRY

When I coach clients I often ask them to create a collage depicting their lives or some aspect of their personal journey at the time. Most are quick to assert, "I'm not an artist." Of course, my cheerful challenge is to help them reconnect with their inner artist—long lost after years of denial. If I'm successful, they discover that in a sense we are all artists. As humans we are, by nature, creative beings. We come into the world equipped to use our imagination to survive, to innovate, and to experience and reveal the beauty and mystery of nature through different mediums.

According to the traditional definition, a true artist is someone who produces a *work* of art. We show deference to such artists, and to the formally designated art mediums they use—song, dance, music, words, painting, sculpting, fashion design, and so forth. Interestingly, we label both the activity and the product as "work." ("He works in stained glass." "She works in metal." "He is a well-known for his artwork.")

Some artists pursue their creations for profit and for sharing beauty with the world. Mikhail Baryshinikov once put it this way: "The essence of all art is to have pleasure in giving pleasure." Others purse their artwork as a hobby for its own sake and for the intrinsic fulfillment it offers the hobbyist.

There is artistry—a spirit of inventiveness—in all of our work. This is true for the architect and the engineer. It is also true for the baker, the chef, and the landscaper. The artisan who crafts furniture or jewelry for sale connects with his or her inner artist. So does the hair stylist whose work as a beautician brings joy to the customer seeking adornment, or the software engineer whose creativity sparks elegant innovations that mystify and make our lives easier.

Can we use the word "artistry" to describe the work of a teacher, a parent, or a physician? What about the youngster at the supermarket checkout counter who figures out on his own that if he is more pleasant than the rest and offers to help customers load groceries into their cars that he might actually generate tips along with goodwill? What about the *con* artist or the *escape* artist? In the broadest sense, an artist is someone who is especially adept at any activity, who uses ingenuity, and who polishes his or her skills toward perfection of that activity.

Work As Toil

In many cultures and social sectors work is "hard labor." In fact, for a majority of the world population, work is synonymous with grueling hours and meager pay. Here too, in America, the working poor must often juggle two minimum wage jobs to make ends meet.

This is not to say that the more privileged are exempt from the experience of work as hardship. In fact, the underbelly of work in just about every sector these days hides a growing dissatisfaction that we cannot ignore. According to the Families and Work Institute, one-third of U.S. employees report feeling chronically overworked, and although 79 percent of them have access to paid vacation time, only 64 percent were able to fit their full vacation time in each year. In fact, Americans log more work hours than any industrial country and average only two weeks vacation, compared to six weeks in Europe. Yet this may well be changing. A recent survey of five thousand British workers reveals similar findings: 60 percent reported they would not be able to make time to take their full vacation.

Work overload is taking a toll. Try to schedule a meeting or connect with a colleague via phone during the workday and you get firsthand confirmation of what the pollsters tell us. We are busier than ever, working as hard as ever. In fact, in October 2005, a group of concerned workers organized a national *Take Back Your Time Day* to protest and draw awareness to our growing problems of overwork. Couple this with an emerging crisis of meaning, where people now seek to connect more fully with the purpose and passion in their work experience and we have conditions that are ripe for the subject of this book.

WORK AS SPIRITUAL PRACTICE

As I write this we are in the midst of working to restore the devastated communities in New Orleans and Biloxi, Mississippi, in the wake of hurricane Katrina. On CNN, I watch the human agony, the tragedy, the desperation of people perched on rooftops and rummaging for food. The rescue teams arrive. A child is plucked to safety into the safe cabin of a helicopter. A military leader takes control, restoring the peace, paving the way for more help to arrive. These are sacred moments where suffering is alleviated by the work of humans. Amidst the pain, the blame, the losses, and the dark uncertainties, we see the Divine emerging: A family is united, and around the country we weep tears of joy for people we have never met. A friend calls to say, "We're safe. We made it to Houston." She tells me the story of her escape—of the human kindness, of those who risked their own lives to help. She repeats the story over and over again, like a mantra, healing her tragedy in the telling of it. We laugh and cry together. We are witnesses, in this moment, to work in its purest, noblest form. I am reminded that work is, in the end, a celebration of the human spirit. It is the lifeblood that courses through our day-to-day existence defining, enriching, and sustaining us.

Matthew Fox's observation in an essay titled "Soul Creation" comes to mind: "All creatures of the universe are busy doing work, and we honor life when we work. The type of work is not important: the fact of work is. All work feeds the soul if it is honest and done to the best of our abilities and if it brings joy to others."

What gets in the way of honest work that "feeds the soul" and "brings joy to others"? Sometimes the daily grind robs us of the time and energy to appreciate work. Work becomes "just a job"—an artificially defined set of tasks we perform for pay. Or it becomes a career—a line of business or occupation we chose for its promise of a good, stable, financially and emotionally rewarding work experience. Either way, work is defined into a narrow set of expectations about what we do to make a living. This job, this career, this occupation often competes with time for inner work—the internal work that's necessary to heal our work in the outer world. And when this happens, work no longer feeds the soul of the worker, even if it brings joy to others.

At other times, our fear gets in the way, deluding us into thinking we have few options before us. Like the recently retired man who regrets his forty years of work, we might spend our entire adulthood immersed in an occupation that is incongruent with our true nature. This man is disconnected from the satisfaction he may have brought his customers. His broken spirit overshadows whatever gratitude he may have felt for a steady income. He faces the end of his life filled with remorse about lost opportunities, missed family moments, and too many moments in a dead end job.

The quality of our work feeds the quality of our life. When we disconnect from the deeper meaning in our work, our lives lack meaning. And while we may be immersed in family and civic affairs, since work commands our best waking hours as adults, a work life devoid of meaning, translates to a "near life" experience. We don't have two lives: a work life and a personal life. We each have one life. And work is the tie that binds our lives and the lives of others together. We work to live, not just in the obvious sense of providing food, clothing, shelter, but in the spiritual sense of expressing our humanity as we raise our families, craft our art, build and rebuild our communities, and search for a meaningful existence.

> "Love and work are the cornerstones of our humanness."
>
> —SIGMUND FREUD

When we approach work as just a job, we rob it of its life affirming nature—of its potential to give. We reduce work to a set of tasks we perform, with a singular intent to get—more pay, more health and retirement benefits, and more time off from work. Work becomes an empty exercise in what Thoreau calls "spending the best part of one's life earning money in order to enjoy a questionable liberty at the end of one's life."

Yet, so many souls work simply to amass enough money to retire. An engineering firm in Pittsburgh has as its vision statement "to make a lot of money." This is also the vision statement for more workers than you'd imagine. And while this is a goal shared by many people, myself included, it is hardly a vision of work and life. This narrow view of the meaning of work sets us up to be perpetually at war within ourselves and with our work. In the next four chapters I will reveal the downside of work, the madness that we must heal if we are to make peace with our work.

INVITATION
How Does Your Work, Work?

Making Peace with Your Work is not an invitation to settle for a dead-end job you hate. In fact, to do so could be detrimental to your physical, emotional, and spiritual well-being. The goal of this book is to encourage you to connect with your present work in a more meaningful way, and if that's not possible, to "make peace" as you leave.

Making peace and making meaning go hand in hand. To come to terms with our work, or revitalize it, we must revisit and examine personal values (such as pride, service, play, humor, mastery, and flexibility). We might also make new choices as we connect more consciously with our purpose and our true selves—pursuing what we feel called to do or what satisfies us, being mindful as we make choices about what we do and how we do it, and weighing the impact of our choices on self and others.

At the end of each chapter in Parts I-III, I will provide "Invitations"—a suggestion or observation followed by questions—to invite you to explore some aspect of your relationship with work, your personal values, or your day-to-day choices at work. I also invite you to start a personal journal in which you will capture your responses to these self-reflective questions.

In Part IV, the last section of the book, I will offer action ideas, rather than questions, this time to invite you to explore possible new choices you might want to make as you renegotiate the terms of engagement with your work.

TWO

The Paradox:
Work Is A Two-Faced Friend

When I ask employees to describe their feelings about work, they offer remarkably bi-polar responses: Work is rewarding, and work is hard. To work is a privilege, but to have to work is a burden. At times the intensity of work leaves little room for creativity, yet under the right conditions, work fires the imagination and nourishes the soul.

Clearly, we are locked in a love-hate dance with our work. Listen to the workplace chatter. We want to earn a good living, but complain about having to go to work. We count the days until retirement, yet fear the prospects of being bored, broke, or marginalized when gainful work ends. We crave the feeling of security work provides, but we rail against the loss of freedom, or the sense of being exploited. We say we enjoy the satisfaction of a job well done, and the thrill of material success. And we are quick to complain about work overload, workplace politics, and low morale.

For me, the work of writing a book is simultaneously the most taxing and the most energizing. It's one of most painful, and definitely among the most pleasurable, life-affirming tasks I have undertaken in my career. This is the paradox of writing a book. This is the paradox of work.

We are simultaneously pulled toward and repelled by the demands of work. Ask any worker what they would do if they won the lottery. "I'd never work again," is the quick reply. But research shows this has not been the case for most lottery winners, or for the extremely well to do, by whatever means. They know what we all secretly know: "nothing works unless we work." For better or worse, work is our friend.

But work is a two-faced friend who both nurtures *and* wounds us. Our basic need to get ahead drives us out of the home and into the workplace, where we do battle with competing demands and beliefs that clash. Our culture teaches us the way to succeed is to make more money, land increasingly responsible positions, and be able to consume more of the best life has to offer. We are eager students, for we want the best home we can buy, the best schools for our kids, the best opportunities that come with the perfect job. Of course for some of us, achieving the best is never enough. Each dream realized is overshadowed by the next big goal. And, if we are really smart, work really hard, or are just plain lucky, we find a way to acquire all the treasures we desire, *and* to shore up substantial savings for our retirement years. This can be costly. In Part III of this book I will discuss why and offer some ideas on a different way to be in relation to our work.

But first, let's look at another paradox of work. While workplace expectations and our approach to work may exact a heavy toll, humanity continues to progress, and our work continues to sustain us well. In many parts of the world our work practices have improved dramatically. There is a growing social consciousness that we can no longer ignore the assaults of worker exploitation, job loss, and work overload. And in many quarters we are working to improve these situations. We also continue to boast awesome achievements in science, medicine, technology, healthcare, the humanities, and the arts.

Still we face the age-old paradox: Can we make a good living, and live a satisfying life? This isn't a question we can ask once, get the answer, and move on. It is a question we must live with as a constant gauge to keep us pointed in the right direction. As I live with this question, some of my notions about work have been shattered altogether. They have begun to crystallize in a new light. I'm more appreciative of the many facets of work—the job we might take as an economic necessity; the hobbies that amuse us, stretch us, and put us in touch with our inner artist or our creative child at play; the voluntary work we do in our community; our work as parents and elders, sons, and daughters; and, most importantly, the inner work we must do if we are to truly make a difference. I'm delighted to share what's emerging. Perhaps it will help shed new light on whatever you are facing in your work.

My view of organizational life has also reformed in positive ways. I see the potential to transform organizations into learning communities where leadership comes not from power *over* another, but rather the power *to* create, collaborate, and serve in ways that matter to humanity. I see emerging workplaces that are rich with promise as one generation passes the leadership baton to the next. Our businesses and institutions are fired-up by new technology and mind-boggling innovations that, if applied with integrity and heart-felt values, can make a difference. I see the rich potential to value people not *in spite of* who they are, but *because of* who they are as we begin to embrace Marshall McLuhan's global village. We are acknowledging for the first time that the "soft stuff is the hard stuff" and that the best laid technical and strategic plans must be complemented by a more conscious attention to people and their potential if we are to succeed.

And, on the shadow side of this promise, I also still see a certain madness. It shows up in our workplaces as tensions we must learn to manage when employer and employee needs collide. Employers want more of our time and creativity and to spend less to get it. Employees want more pay, more time off, and more alternatives that satisfy life balance needs. We crave more leisure, and our jobs demand more of our time. We long for more freedom or autonomy, and this longing clashes with organizational demands. We hang on nonetheless because the job puts food on the table, even if it leaves our souls starved.

Carl Jung once wrote: "When the individual does not become conscious of his inner contradictions, the world must perforce act out the conflict and be torn in opposite halves." Because our workplaces and communities are extensions of each of us, our inner struggles show up *systemically* as well. Our workplaces worldwide are riddled with impossible polarities and competing demands. We extol the value of teamwork, but reward people based on individual achievement. We encourage people to take risks and innovate, while taking a stance that mistakes are intolerable. We invite workers to think strategically, but allow no time to stop and reflect. We say we support family-friendly work environments, while we demand longer hours and intensify workloads. In the larger global community, we witness both the suffering of oppressed workers and the good fortune of the free. We are simultaneously saddened by the plight of the unemployed or underpaid and inspired by the privilege and prowess of the overpaid.

Awareness and resolution of these polarities are the keys to *Making Peace with Your Work.* So how do we *make peace?* There are many options we will explore throughout this book. At times peace is simply the absence of struggle. We let go of the war dance and forgive the past, opening ourselves to the possibility of restored trust. We come to terms with a person or situation. We reach an agreement that satisfies our needs and the needs of the other party. We release hard feelings, bury the hatchet, declare a truce, or call a cease-fire. We reconcile our differences and restore harmony. At times peace is the reconciliation between opposing forces, most notably our outer work and our inner work. At times it's simply letting go of old assumptions that no longer serve us. Making peace with our work ultimately requires replacing some old rules we lived by with new ones of our own making.

"Are you suggesting we should turn the other cheek and just put up with whatever happens at work?" A very frustrated airline employee who had just endured a pay cut coupled with an increased workload recently put this question to me. Well, yes—at first. Before we can change a thing, it helps to *know* it. Work is a two-faced friend. To nurture your relationship with a sometimes difficult friend, you must first accept her—come to know her *as she is*. Once we extend this unconditional regard, we can practice forgiveness, and begin the process of healing our differences. Likewise, we must first appreciate the paradoxical nature of our work—whatever that work may be. We must learn to celebrate the gifts of work, even as we address the hardships work may pose. A good example of the importance of this attitude can be found among colleagues in my field. Those of us who do anti-oppression work risk burning out on anger and frustration if we only focus on what's broken. To be truly effective long term, we must come to understand that differences may polarize us, but it's our common humanity that heals us. Making peace with our work inevitably requires us to balance the polarities of activist and healer. We must hold in our consciousness the transcendent goodness of humanity and the gains we have made, as we work vigorously to move against injustice. This is the stance towards work and towards social change that endeared us to great leaders like Mahatma Gandhi and Dr. Martin Luther King, Jr.

Does *Making Peace* mean looking for the moments of joy, creativity, and transcendence where your work makes a difference in someone's life? Often it does. And if you're thinking, "There is *no way* that's possible in my job!" you may find the tools and ideas in the chapters that follow helpful.

Is *Making Peace* about putting up with a job while doing something more meaningful in your community or with your family? Does it come from choosing to be okay with your choice to work hard in the first half of your life at whatever work you find in order to store up enough financial resources to retire and do something fun and meaningful in the second half? Does it mean finding your life purpose and pursuing that, or does it mean quitting a heartbreaking job and moving on? For different people in different situations it could mean any or all of the above. Ultimately, what we seek is resolution of the dissonance between where we are and where we'd like to be. But to make right choices about what to do and where to do it, we must first get clear about how to *be*—how we want to show up in our work world.

Put simply, *Making Peace* begins with a particular attitude. It's a stance we take in relation to work. Even if your work is fabulous and you are perfectly suited to it, you might still need to make peace with your work by consciously acknowledging and celebrating your good fortune. We are products of a culture that tends to highlight the downside of things—and not just in broadcast news. The typical response I get from people who are engaged in work that really works for them is, "I love my work, but...." They then give more attention to the "buts" than to what's right with their work. Yes, there will always be room for improvement behind the "buts"—more pay, fewer grueling hours, a more enlightened boss, a shorter commute, more freedom to create, less politics, fewer competing demands, more stability. This list goes on.

When we make peace, we shift our focus from the downside of work to an inner focus on how to connect with work in a more uplifting, more spiritually rewarding way. We lay our egos down and open our hearts to the possibility there is goodness in the world, in our workplaces, in each other. We also open our eyes to the harsh realities of work and come to terms with what we see, by linking the outer challenges of duty, sacrifice, service to our inner work on passion, purpose, gratitude, and self-affirming choices.

A couple years ago, I enrolled in Dr. Barry Johnson's seminar on Polarity Management™. Johnson teaches us to examine whether our seemingly unsolvable problems are not problems at all with a "right solution," but polarities (or paradoxes), which must be managed. Polarities to be managed require us to tap what Jim Collins and Jerry Porras label, "the genius of the *and*." This awareness has changed my life. I am learning to be more accepting of the contradictions in people and situations. It has given me a new set of tools for transcending difficulties and resolving both internal and interpersonal conflicts. Most importantly, Johnson's work reminds us to examine the upsides *and* the downsides of a situation, to search for the important outcomes that can resolve both polarities.

Ultimately, what gets in the way of making peace with our work, is a lack of awareness that work, like life, is paradox. When we make peace, we become comfortable with paradox. We learn to look with new eyes at our relationship with work, to see both the light *and* the shadow side of this constant companion. Our work is neither good *nor* bad. Our work is both good *and* bad. Instead of approaching the hard parts of our work as problems to be solved we learn to see these as polarities—contradictions on our work—to be managed.

If work has two faces, so does our relationship with it. Our soul's desire for freedom, autonomy, and time to stop, reflect, and nurture ourselves is at odds with the physical and emotional demands of work in a world that is increasingly complex, increasingly challenging.

Transcendence requires that we constantly ask questions: How can I find meaning in what I'm doing? What lesson is my work life trying to teach me? Am I doing what I'm called to do at this point in my life? It requires knowing when to push and when to pull, when to hold on and when to let go. The story that follows illustrates this well:

BETSY PICKREN'S STORY:
"Holding On, Letting Go"

Years ago I left an organization where I had worked for fifteen years to start a new position as partner in another organization. It was a new beginning, so I was anxious to please. The harder I tried, the less of "me" was available.

As I tried to impress, I found myself making more and more choices that were inconsistent with what I knew to be true for me. I also found, ironically, that the more I focused on pleasing my new colleagues, the more I lost my ability to please them. Eventually my ceaseless striving began to impact my work with clients. I was losing myself. I began to question whether I was even in the right business. In the end, things fell apart and I severed the relationship.

This experience is in contrast to another where, as vice president of client services, we faced the question of whether to consolidate two units. I was clear that we weren't ready. I set out to advocate for the position I felt was right, but quickly decided that perhaps it wasn't worth the struggle. As I was about to give up, one of my colleagues gave me a gift—a stuffed pink pig with the inscription, "sometimes the only way out is through the muddle." Encouraged by these words of support, I went in the next day, did everything in my power to influence the group, and was successful.

I share these two examples because they taught me much about managing the tension between endless struggle and letting go at work. I learned that the endless struggle in an effort to control the uncontrollable becomes a problem when you keep fighting long after the good or the usefulness of your efforts ceases. And I learned there is also a downside to letting go prematurely. If you give up too soon you miss the opportunities that come from prevailing. This tension between knowing when to hold on tenaciously and knowing when to let go is at the heart of our work and our work relationships.

Betsy's story is exemplified daily in our workplaces. As we manage these polarities we must become conscious of what happens at the extreme poles where ceaseless striving can lead to burnout or where letting go prematurely can amount to not caring enough.

We must also be aware of the possibility of holding a "both/and" stance, not just an "either/or" stance as we manage our relationship with work. Several years ago my firm conducted an employee satisfaction survey for a children's hospital. Employees' complaints were escalating and management, fearing this might have a negative impact on patient care, wanted to take the pulse of the workforce. Shockingly, employees scored off the charts on job satisfaction. Our consultants and the hospital management were pleased at the good news, but thoroughly baffled, given the force of the criticisms about other aspects of their work culture. So we scheduled focus groups to get at the stories behind the high job satisfaction scores. One nurse's comments sums up the sentiments of the entire staff, "At the end of the day, my feet hurt and I'm still ticked off about many of the changes the new administration is making. Yet I want to be here. I look into the children's eyes, and I know I've made a difference. This is the best work possible."

Does this mean it is easier for people in helping professions, such as paramedics, teachers, social workers, or Red Cross volunteers to make peace with their work? No. I believe we all have the potential to connect with the deeper meaning in our work, as this nurse has done. But this is difficult, because the romantic ideal we seek constantly butts up against the harsh realities of a work world that in some ways is increasingly insane.

Living with paradox teaches us to forgive—to make peace with—the inconsistencies in our work. Like my client Ken, the office politics may frustrate you *and* your work continues to be satisfying, for it touches lives in significant ways. Your workplace may be going through a really nasty transition that leaves you stressed out and upset these days, *and* you still are sure you're doing the right work in the right place, so you remain committed for the long haul. At the end of the day you can be satisfied with the contribution you have made, *and* still find yourself wondering if this work is truly what you're called to do.

In working on my career and working through this book, I have come to accept—to make peace with—the paradoxes inherent in my own work. I am aware of the backbreaking task of hauling luggage as I dash to make an airline connection, *and* I am grateful to be doing this work. I see the disappointment in my grandchildren's eyes as they cry "Nnena you're leaving again?" It throws me back twenty years to a missed baseball game when my son posed the same sad question. I feel the pain. *And* I live for the joyous greeting on my return when, like happy puppies, they circle me jumping and clapping "Nnena, Nnena! You're back! We missed you!" I cringe at the routine tasks of filing expense receipts, billing, scheduling, and keeping track of tons of detail. *And* I smile with pride and gratitude when the payoffs come—the thank you notes, the check in the mail, the tear-filled eyes of the man who hangs around after my seminar to say, "It was like you were speaking to me, specifically! You've made a difference."

I am learning to remain conscious of the power of the *and* as my work weaves back and forth like a figure eight between its polarities. The nail-biting drudgery of crafting a proposal gives way to the euphoria of winning the contract. The tension of laboring through a tedious project evaporates with the exhilaration of breakthrough results. I take it all in as part of the whole, and I am grateful.

To come to terms with work, or any situation for that matter, we must understand it and accept it in all of its complexities. This means being willing to live with paradox, and to use a lens of *both/and*, rather than *either/or* to examine our experience of it. In the exercise at that follows I invite you to experiment with seeing your work this way.

INVITATION
See Your Work for ALL That It Is

In his book *Polarity Management*, Dr. Barry Johnson teaches us that sometimes seeming problems to be solved are really polarities to be managed. A problem can usually be solved by applying the one right solution. A polarity, in contrast, is ongoing and its opposite poles are interdependent so there is no one simple solution.

Workers juggle such dilemmas every day. In one factory where I worked, employees complained about having to put in overtime and, when given the chance to opt out, no one wanted to give up the extra pay. As a writer, my solitary work is a delightful, creative outlet and it becomes lonely and isolating.

If I open my boundaries and invite others in for long periods, my writing suffers. If I close my boundaries and devote myself earnestly to writing, the isolation sets in. To manage the paradoxes of our work we must move back and forth between such polarities, attempting to maximize the upside (in my, case creative expression), while minimizing the downside (isolation).

In the space below, or in your journal, capture an upside—or positive feature—of your work AND its downside—or drawback—at the opposite pole.

_____and_____

_____and_____

_____and_____

_____and_____

Next, select one of the pairs you created and write, in your journal, answers to the following questions:

1. How can I lessen the downside of these opposite poles?

2. How can I maximize the benefits of the upside?

PART II

The Madness:
Three Questions to Ponder

THREE

Are You Working in The War Zone?

Often, the marriage of worker and work is a rocky one, riddled with tensions and paradoxes. The morning commute, the performance reviews that can make or break a career, the long night shift, the job interviews that can make or break your future, the dank climate of the coal mines, the tensions between a nurse and doctor, the children with guilt-evoking eyes as you run out the front door on your way to work, the downsizings dubbed "the drive-by shootings of corporate America" by a Wall Street journalist. These are the harsh realities.

The title of this chapter was inspired by Joe, an IT specialist who has been a self-described casualty of outsourcing three times, with three different companies, in six years. Here is Joe's story:

JOE REYNOLDS' STORY:
"Shell-Shocked"

I was recruited away from a job that I enjoyed and that I was successful at. But I was ready to move on to pursue a position that offered more career opportunities. I had "topped out." I was reporting directly to the chief information officer along with three other guys; all of them were more senior than me. Besides, I have no interest in managing. I like the technical work. So when a friend mentioned that there was a good opportunity where she worked, I applied and they hired me immediately. They were very excited about what I would bring to the table.

Eighteen months into the new job, they sold the company, and I was "excessed." I was furious, shell-shocked, confused—I mean, didn't they know this was coming when they hired me? I hadn't been around long enough to get any of the "bennies" of being severed. I had just gotten married, we had bought a brand new home, my wife and I were expecting our first child, we had two car notes, a mortgage, she was in between jobs, and we had decided she should wait until after the baby was born to go back to work, so the healthcare benefits and everything else rested on my job. Now here I was—jobless.

I panicked and took the first IT-related job I could find that offered good healthcare benefits. I won't bore you with all the gory details, but two years later—here we go again. "We're outsourcing IT overseas" or something like that. This time I hit rock bottom. I dragged my feet for six months while Cynthia, my wife, carried the load. She had just landed a job with Ohio State University. I stayed home with our toddler. Every morning I'd get up and go sit in front of the computer combing the Internet, looking for work, looking for ideas, whatever. Things got tense in my marriage. Cynthia accused me of not really seriously looking for a job, and I got defensive. Of course she was right. I guess I was just plain depressed.

I eventually got it together and landed my current job. Guess what? Now they're talking about "consolidating" my area. I know what that means. I feel like I'm working in the war zone. You never know when you're going to be hit. This time, I've started my own business on the side, just in case.

Thrown off center by the drama of work overload, serial downsizing and restructuring, economic uncertainties and constant change, our relationship with work can easily become strained. When this happens, we might don a self-protective armor declaring, "It's just a job." Or we might simply lie low, crouching in the shadows, withholding the best we have to offer, and playing it safe until things get better. A few leave, but most persist, even if they feel powerless or stuck. And the work goes on.

Once at work, the talk is of business wars, the ever-toughening competition, and the need to strategize in order to win. No sector is exempt. If we hire into health care, we find a work world at war with itself as it responds to the challenge of providing access to safe, reliable, low-cost, high-quality patient care in a climate of turbulence, competition, and complex battles between providers and health care insurers. Banking, retail, manufacturing, academic, and governmental sectors all face similar work-related conundrums. Even not-for-profit agencies that seek to heal our culture must compete fiercely against each other for shrinking streams of philanthropic dollars.

The literature on work/life balance likes to tout statistics that dramatize the consequences of being at war with work. They tell us "most heart attacks occur at 9:00 am on Mondays on the job." The language of managers and scholars who examine the impact of today's climate of mergers and downsizing does the same. They label employees who leave as "casualties" and describe the workers who remain as the "working wounded" who suffer from "survivor syndrome." If metaphors give us insights about the psyche of a culture, then surely, our work culture is a war zone.

Listening to my clients at work, I am struck by how often battle images come up. Many compare their business climate to combative sports. When they turn to nature for analogies, they choose terms like "permanent white water," or "the tsunami effect" to describe their turbulent work places. Peaceful images of work like sowing seeds and harvesting grain, giving birth to ideas, or creating foundations for survival, growth, and sustainability come later, or as afterthoughts, or with much coaxing from a facilitator who seeks to teach balance and inspire.

Best-selling business books advise us to *Swim with The Sharks,* or to *Do Lunch or Be Lunch.* To be successful we are told, we must don our work helmets in the spirit of winning. Conventional wisdom teaches us that work is a battle of wits, where the brightest and the best win and others may be losers. It matters little whether the work has to do with flipping burgers, driving buses, building buildings, or planning ways to get the most out of people. Our work pits us against each other in competitive games in which there are winners and losers, high achievers and low achievers, promotions and firings. We cut costs, cut budgets, cut people. If we survive the cuts, we double our efforts, bragging about our work ethic as we wait anxiously for the next axe to fall.

Recently, I conducted a series of employee focus groups following a merger that resulted in significant changes and job loss. The company hired me to take the pulse of the surviving workforce because they feared morale was low. They were right. Angry and disillusioned, employees painted scenarios in which senior management was the enemy and where the employees live daily with the threat of outsourcing, job loss, work overload, and having to get better results faster with less time. Some worried out loud about whether their candor would eventually cost them their jobs. Having to combat feelings of powerlessness and vulnerability in their workplace, they were emotionally at war with their work.

Years ago, I made a similar observation as I consulted with a medical facility where we invited a group of interns to reflect on their medical school experience. They described the model of learning as based on survival of the fittest, often with few safety nets. "How ironic," one of them pointed out, "that we are being prepared to be healers using a military model."

Yet for many workers, these escalating expectations can be as tantalizing as they are taxing. In spite of the challenges of our intense work world, we delight in the satisfaction of a job well done. We want to excel. Most of us enter our workplaces eager to learn and contribute and be fairly compensated. We want to progress and we are seduced by the promise of growth-producing, wealth-producing, satisfying work. Motivation theorists have told us for decades what fires our imaginations and captures our commitment at work. Beyond being compensated well for what we do, we want to achieve—to excel at what we do. We want autonomy and recognition for our efforts. We also want what Abraham Maslow described in his Hierarchy of Needs: survival, safety, affiliation, esteem, and ultimately self-actualization where we become all that we can be.

Our employers understand this. When they court us, they assure us that this is a place where we can make a meaningful contribution, take on increasing amounts of responsibility, earn good money, and retire happy. Many people fulfill this dream—some in their place of employment, others by striking out on their own. In either case, these people will tell you they love their work and they enjoy the challenge of exceeding their own and others' expectations.

But for just as many people there comes a point where we are wounded by our work. We buckle under the competing demands of work and family. We burn out on stretch goals. Our voice is silenced by the politics of our workplace. Our morale and our performance falter. Sometimes this happens because something in the leadership approach, the work environment, or the work itself disappoints us. Sometimes it is because we fail to take good care of our selves. In either case this wounding takes a toll. Our relationship with work becomes loveless and we begin to look askance at what we're doing and where we're doing it.

As the invitation that follows suggests, it helps if we are aware of where the wounds occur in our work so we can make conscious choices aimed at self care.

INVITATION
Commit to Making Peace
with Your Work

Most of us have some aspect of our work with which we are at odds. It could be the stress-provoking morning commute, dissatisfaction with a boss whose leadership is lacking, having to do battle with a large bureaucracy in order to get things done, or the constant bombardment of work overload and impossible deadlines.

Depending on our stance and the choices we make, these daily assaults can be minor annoyances that come with the turf or they can inflict life-threatening wounds. For example, the worker who seizes the morning commute as a time to indulge in fun, informative books on tape is having a different experience from the worker who approaches the commute with dread and loathing. The worker who learns to leverage the power of good one-on-one relationships and transparent communication across organizational boundaries can get things done with a lot fewer headaches than the one who despairs, insisting "it can't be done, the politics won't let us."

In your journal, explore the following:

1. Where do I do battle with my work?
2. Where am I wounded?
3. How can I change my stance going forward?
3. What actions can I take to promote a more healing presence in these areas of my work?

FOUR

Are You Working in The Fast Lane?

In the summer of 2000, I was privileged to share a keynote spot at the annual Organization Development Network conference with Alan Webber, founder of *Fast Company* magazine. Together we extolled the virtues of creating organizations that are fast, flat, friendly, and flexible. What was neat and unique about the format for our presentation, is that Webber, who was hundreds of miles away at another event, was instantaneously beamed via teleconference onto a large screen behind the podium where I stood on stage at the Atlanta Hilton. Our efficient high tech extravaganza was warmly received by admiring conferees. As the initial applause died down, we invited questions from the audience. Webber and I continued to vibe together interpersonally and electronically, fielding questions back and forth from our very enthusiastic audience. The last question came from a well-known change management specialist in the audience. Her query was a simple, provocative one that gave me pause: *"What's wrong with slow?"* she asked.

I have been thinking about that question since that day. Could it be that we are evolving into a culture where speed is in and contemplation is out? Could it be that in our haste to get better results faster and faster we are losing our ability to have measured, meaningful dialogue? In the workplaces I visit, employees clearly work in the speed zone. Ask them, and they will tell you there is typically too much to do and too little time in a given workday. In our clock-driven, data-laden workplaces we praise the efficiency of the multi-tasker and measure success in terms of productivity, even as we pay lip service to excellence, creativity, and strategic thinking—all of which tend to take more time. We value swift action and have little patience for those who pause to ponder. Such behavior is seen as dawdling, even if it allows us to pause in order to gather our wits, or to let difficulties blow over, as they sometimes do.

THE PROMISE AND THE PITFALLS OF SPEED

But speed is not without its virtues. We live in a time when innovation and speed give us the global competitive edge in business, government, and other sectors as well. And we have been rising steadily to the challenge. Over the past three years, American productivity growth has risen about 5 percent. Working with organizations, I often sit at the conference table with decision makers who must act with haste to shore up market share and productivity as profits slip away.

> "Even if you win the rat race, you're still a rat."
>
> —LILY TOMLIN

I also log many hours helping organizations decipher the emerging values of the newest members of their work-force—the twenty-something-year-olds who have little patience for routine, superficial work. The well-educated new entrants I typically work with are bright, eager, techno-savvy individuals who are anxious to get ahead, to learn, to grow, and to make a good living. They want meaningful assignments, and hanker for stretch goals. And they want these *now*.

It isn't surprising that these new entrants have a sense of urgency and hold different expectations than previous generations whose pact with the workplace was "take care of me and you will have my loyalty." Millennials, as these members of Generation Y are sometimes called, have come along at a time when the workplace promise of security is a dim memory. They know they must take responsibility for their own career, their own pension plans, and their ongoing education in a world where knowledge becomes rapidly obsolete. Their allegiance to an employer, when it exists, is conditional—"show me you care and you will earn my loyalty." They know that these days there are no guarantees of security. They must move quickly to build a secure future and they must be ready to move on—to change gears swiftly—if things change.

Interestingly the new workforce is itself a product of a culture of speed. Millennials grew up with non-stop stimulation and were likely highly scheduled from the time they entered grade school. They are used to being armed with cell phones, instant messaging, computer games, iPods, and the ever-present media. Many are masters at multi-tasking, capable of doing school work (or office work) with the television on, streaming simultaneous visual, aural, and verbal data while instant messages pop in by computer or cell phone and music plays into the earpiece of an iPod. Not surprisingly, at work they crave the "now-ness" to which they've grown accustomed. While the older work force may be frustrated by the constant changes, millennials are invariably frustrated by a work world they feel grinds too slowly. Of course, from the organization's viewpoint, the potential gift in this is that it feeds our growing penchant for speed.

There are many situations where speed is sanctioned. When a national or international disaster strikes, for example, we very appropriately cry out for a speedy response. Just in the past year, I can still recall the haunting pictures of people across the world clinging to life and hoping for speed in the aftermath of catastrophes such as a tsunami, earthquakes, hurricanes, and coal mine disasters.

The problem with speed comes only when it becomes taken for granted as a way of life—when speed becomes a deeply embedded cultural value that leaves little room for other ways of being. In one of my culture audit exercises, I ask workers to pick an animal that represents their workplace or their work team. These days the top picks are fast, ferocious, or cunning animals: lions, bears, foxes, and tigers. Animals that are fast, focused, and ferocious come to mind because our definition and experience of work centers on getting the most done, usually in a steady and intense way, often in a rushed and harried way. It takes intense energy, and a lot of it, to get through our workday, and our work climates are being defined by this reality.

There is much in our broader culture that mirrors this obsession with speed. In recent years, I have noticed a shift in the behavior of theater goers. Several minutes before the final curtain comes down, people anxiously begin to leave. They want to beat the crowd. You see it clearly in the set of the jaw that says, "I must not get trapped in the line that is filing out of the theater. I must not get stuck slowly meandering out of the parking lot." What's the rush? There is no time clock for the Sunday evening matinee, no deadline to meet. Sadly, there is no longer room for the long goodbye because our instincts now tell us fast is always better.

I also see this when, on occasion, I must join the morning commute on Highway 285 in Atlanta where I live. Timidly I enter the speed zone of frenetic workers and their automobiles. Jarred awake by the blare of the alarm clock an hour or so before joining the fray, the commuters drive to work with the intensity and focus of the embattled. I imagine those who make it safely to their destinations charge forward with the same resolve to begin a daily drill of marching from task to task, meeting to meeting, setting goals, and making the numbers.

Like good soldiers, most are not aware of the meaning in this madness, for at work there is little time for reflection. Most do not enjoy the luxury of stopping to savor moments of transcendence at work—a life saved, a breakthrough, a customer's load made lighter. Instead they forge ahead counting the minutes until quitting time, when they return to the madness of the commute, the second shift of homework, bills, anxiety-provoking TV news, family crises, and finally bedtime, marked by the setting of the alarm clock for the next day's work.

Schoolteachers rush against the bell to meet curriculum goals for each day. They are pressed to bring everyone up to speed in twenty-minute segments punctuated by the bell. Those students who lag behind are problems to be solved, and even the most humane, people-centered educators who take the time to nurture young minds and enliven their students' spirits are ultimately judged on whether their charges scored at the right levels on standardized tests. These goals and tests are indeed important. They prepare students for the reality of the work world. They serve as a gauge for present and future success and provide useful feedback that can be used to adjust instructional approaches and provide additional support so that no child is ultimately "left behind." But when I conduct in-service training sessions with educators, they tell me the work climate and the pressure to teach to the test rather than to student needs or curiosity is their greatest source of frustration.

Shift workers in manufacturing facilities are no different from teachers in this respect; neither are physicians, nurses, project managers, salespeople, government employees, lawyers, or servers in restaurants. All share in common the workday pressures associated with getting the job done efficiently. Implicitly or explicitly, work is about beating the clock, out-producing the best, and making the numbers. Recently we have upped the ante once again. We have gone beyond setting goals to setting *stretch* goals and beyond meeting expectations to *exceeding* them. The emerging norms are the more the better, the faster the better, and the better the better.

Carl Honoré has written a thoughtful book titled *In Praise of Slowness: How a Worldwide Movement is Challenging the Cult of Speed*. In it he cites compelling evidence that this maddening pace of our work world is fueling increased drug abuse as employees turn to stimulants (beyond coffee) to compensate for lack of sufficient sleep and to keep pace with the demands of work. In fields ranging from nursing to IT, burnout and the accompanying slump in employee morale are emerging as top management concerns. A 2005 study of IT managers surveyed by Meta Group, an IT staffing and compensation research firm, found that over 71 percent cited employee burnout as a serious issue affecting productivity and turnover. As Honoré suggests, when everyone is going fast, fast no longer offers an advantage.

Of course this discussion is not to suggest that we should get into the slow lane and stall. It is simply a reminder that we must find ways to balance speed with slowness, for in our breathless haste we run the risk of losing time for the long strategic look forward, and miss the simple joy in being fully present in the moment.

The quiz that follows will help you discover where you might benefit from shifting down.

INVITATION
Are You Working In the Fast Lane?

How often do you	Always	Often	Sometimes	Almost Never	Never
1. Keep working on your computer while a coworker tries to talk with you?					
2. Order the check while you're eating dessert so no time is wasted?					
3. Leave a performance before the final curtain call so you can beat others out of the theater (or stadium)?					
4. Eat lunch while tapping at the computer keyboard and talking on the phone?					
5. Get fidgety if you sit for more than ten minutes doing absolutely nothing?					
6. Drive ten MPH above the speed limit?					
7. Mindlessly turn the TV on as soon as you enter your home?					
8. Rush from one task to the next at work without stopping to reflect on what you've just done or are about to do next?					
9. Make promises you can't keep because your plate is too full?					
10. Experience a personal event such as a wedding or unexpected visit from a friend or family member as an "interruption" of your work schedule?					
11. Eat a meal so quickly you really didn't taste any of it?					
12. Leave one meeting mid-point to catch another meeting that is already under way?					
13. Feel annoyed at a customer whose phone call or visit is taking up too much of your time?					

If you answered "always" or "often" to three or more of these questions, chances are good you are working in the fast lane. The good news is you have also just identified a couple of behaviors that you can simply choose to modify as you begin to practice shifting down to get better long-term results.

In your journal make note of one or two of these items you want to modify. Share your plan with someone close to you and ask them to help you monitor the change.

FIVE

Do You Bring Your Inner Self To Work?

Brenton Williams slowly puts his phone back on the receiver. He had just received the call he feared. Laddie, his golden retriever, has to be euthanized tomorrow. Brenton is heartbroken. But there is no time to think about this now. George, his manager, is waiting for him. He grabs a notepad and dashes off to meet with George. As he leaves, his eyes rest briefly on the photograph of his runaway daughter, Jean. She is in Denver somewhere. He knows this only because she has maxed out his credit card, and the charge card company has made it clear he has to pay up the $5,000 bill because she is, after all, an authorized user.

He arrives at George's office. It's bad news. "I've got to give you the heads up," George says. "You've been a real prize employee, so you deserve to know what's going down." Through a foggy blur Brenton hears George saying something about the possibility of Brenton's job being eliminated in three to four months. He thanks George.

He doesn't know why. He grabs his notepad and staggers out the door, bumping into Shirley, one of his colleagues. "Hey, Brenton! How're doing?" "Great, just *great!*" his strategic self gushes automatically, flashing a too broad smile as he bounces energetically back into his office.

Inside, he feels like a dead man walking. As the poem cited in the introduction put it, his soul craves stopping. Brenton's thoughts race. Questions file through his mind:

> *What am I doing here? How come I felt more relieved than sad, when George gave me the news about possibly being put out of work? I've been ready to move on for years now. I wonder what kind of severance they'll offer if my job is eliminated. Hopefully, it will be substantial enough so I can take some time off. I might even hire one of those life coaches. Maybe I can find my daughter, Jean, and make peace with her. Maybe this will be my chance to work in a different sector, or go back to school and try something else. I graduated college then fell into this job unsure about myself and my choice. I was so young then. Now I have a better sense of my strengths and interests.*

He slides into his chair and logs onto his computer. Soon he is clicking away at the keyboard generating bar charts and recommendations for an important project. His report will be done by quitting time. Brenton will be on a plane to London tomorrow ready to deliver a detailed, compelling PowerPoint version of the report to his client.

Our Outer, Social Self

Brenton is no different from the rest of us. At work he plays to his outer self, the part of himself that is strategic, performance-oriented, socially conforming, smart, and winning. There is an aspect of this outer self that incorporates what psychologists call the idealized self—how we would like to be seen by others and who we would like to become. The outer self dresses for success, comes to work on time, gets it right, says things clearly, and generally comes across well—competitive, expert, and ambitious. Yet ironically this self is motivated primarily by fear: fear of separation from our livelihood; fear of looking foolish, losing face, failing to achieve goals, not making the numbers, or being vulnerable in a host of ways that will be explored later in this book.

The ego (or personality) is a product of this external self. Our ego serves us well in the external world. It protects us by deluding us into thinking we are perfect, or ought to be. *It is concerned with doing and becoming and is, therefore, future oriented.* It fuels our drive to learn, to perform, to achieve success, or to act in ways that conform to what others expect of us. This external, ego-based self wants to look good, wants to be smart, and is driven to win. Not surprisingly, this is the persona that our organizations hire and reward.

Our Inner, True Self

Our inner self—our soul (or essence) is centered in the now. It is our true self—who we are in essence. Unlike our external self, which is performance-oriented (concerned with doing), our inner self is reflection-oriented (concerned with being). It may be incorrect to say our inner self is motivated in any particular way since the term motivation connotes goal-orientedness rather than simply being. But for the purposes of this discussion, we could say that, in a sense, the inner self is "motivated" by purpose. This self wants to create a fuller experience of the time we have to live. It is the self that is willing to be authentic, even if to do so makes us unpopular at times. It is the self that seeks connection with higher ideals, that is generous in empowering others, and that shows compassion for self and for the world. Our inner self is truly courageous, not in the sense of winning or looking good, but in the sense of being willing to risk failing. To borrow from the work of Warren Bennis and Bert Nanus: where the outer self seeks to "do things right" in the external world, the inner self seeks to "do the right things" for your soul.

In conventional workplaces, these two selves are often forced to do battle. The external self tends to win out, because the behaviors associated with this self get rewarded. In the process, our souls—our inner selves—cry out for expression, even sending physical cues that we tend to ignore.

What I find most disturbing is this means we are not just at war with our work, we are also at war *within* ourselves at work as these two aspects of us compete for air time.

INVITATION
Seek Alignment Between Your Inner and Outer Selves

When Mrs. Rosa Parks refused to give up her seat on the bus, she resolved an inner crisis of integrity. She made a bold choice that brought her outer behaviors into alignment with her inner beliefs.

Pay attention when your outer (strategic) self collides with your inner (true) self—when what you are doing, or how you are behaving, is different from what is right and true for you.

In your journal explore the following:

1. What things are you saying yes to while feeling no in your gut?

2. Make a list of three areas at work where you would benefit from bringing your outer behaviors into greater alignment with your true feelings.

3. Explore some specific choices you could make in each case.

PART III

Inner Work:
The Path to Making Peace

"We all run on two clocks. One is the outside clock, which ticks away our decades and brings us ceaselessly to the dry season. The other is the inside clock, where you are your own timekeeper and determine your own chronology, your own internal weather, and your own rate of living. Sometimes the inner clock runs itself out long before the outer one, and you see a dead man going through the motions of living."

—MAX LERNER

SIX

The Practice of Stopping

It's been said that music resides not in the note itself, but in the space between the notes. The same holds true for work. It's in stopping to reflect that we learn the most. When we stop and journey inward, we create a space to reflect. We can, as Rilke put it, "Be and yet know the great void where all things begin." In this void we pause to gather up the wisdom hidden in the hardships and the triumphs of our work and our lives. We refuel ourselves with renewed energy and clarity for the continued journey.

But introspection is no simple task. Work, by its very nature, pulls us outside of ourselves into the outer world of action. We have deadlines to meet, student loans to repay, a new baby to feed, first car, first home, and daily sustenance to consider. The rush hour madness draws our attention outward as we hurry to catch the school bus, make our train connections, or negotiate traffic on our way to school or work. Once there, we immerse ourselves in the demands of the external world, relentlessly moving from task to task until day's end. Then, exhausted, we repeat the process: rush hour, homework, personal relationships, bills to be paid, and the daily (bad) news all compete for our attention as the day winds to a close. We bog down in the persistent turmoil of a workplace that is morphing at maddening speed, and demanding more of our time. What often gets lost in the fray is our inner life.

Yet, intuitively we know that stopping is good for us. We spend a good deal of time thinking about stopping, even if we don't allow ourselves to act on it. We think about the end of work. When is quitting time? At what age will I retire? What do I want my next job to be? Secretly some of us want to say to our bosses, "I just want to stop for a while, perhaps a few days, perhaps a couple of years—who knows?" And, of course, there is vacation time. We spend the better part of our work year planning for a couple of weeks off when we can simply stop. We are preoccupied with stopping because it enables us to empty and nourish ourselves so our reentry into the fray of daily duties and life struggles can be made lighter.

Years ago I worked with the Kaleel Jamison Consulting Group. My mentors there taught me about the power of stopping as a way to reflect on our work activities, gather up the learnings—what worked, what didn't, what did we learn—and then plan how to integrate those lessons in the next go around. They coached managers and other workers to take breaks after each major activity, perhaps leave the desk and walk around the building in silence, reflecting and connecting with inner wisdom. That training has been a gift for me.

Think of all the creative ways you can apply this to your work life. For instance you may find, as I have, that mini vacations every six weeks do a lot more for the soul than a single two—or three—week stretch each year. Stopping after each activity or encounter at work is a great exercise. It allows us to rest, relax, and consciously assimilate the lessons of that experience before going on to the next task. Stress management experts have long taught us that such breaks are a more powerful antidote to stress than long periods off infrequently.

Research also shows that stopping to debrief your activities and encounters immediately after completion is more likely to result in positive change. It allows you to appreciate yourself and your work and to integrate key lessons in a conscious and lasting way. It's also a great stress reliever. After each major task or interpersonal encounter at work, stop and take several deep, cleansing breaths. Then answer the following questions:

1. What went *well* and why?
2. What do I plan to *keep* doing based on this experience?
3. What do I plan to *start*, or *stop*, doing based on this experience?

A friend of mine works as a technical support specialist at Hewlett Packard. His workdays are spent walking frustrated customers through the paces of making peace with their computers. Invariably his clients are tense, frustrated, and work-weary. They call tech support as a last resort. His job is to offer accurate effective solutions.

Recently this technical support specialist called me for a bit of career advice. "In my performance review today, my boss said, 'You're *really strange*. The stress of this job doesn't seem to faze you at all.' Should I take her comment as a compliment?" Here is his story. You be the judge.

VINCENT BROWN'S STORY:
"Stopping to Exhale at Work"

I deal with frustrated callers all day. Their voices become louder, then shrill. Sometimes they toss off an expletive or two. By the time I get to my eighth caller in forty-five minutes, I can feel my shoulders becoming tense. This is my cue to stop. I can't walk away from my workstation. But I've taught myself how to stop—how to disengage so that I can continue to serve in a polite and helpful way.

I wasn't always able to do this. But several years ago I signed up for a martial arts class and learned the principles of chi gong, an ancient Chinese healing practice that dates back five thousand years. It's all about how I use my breath—my life force. When I face an irate customer, I follow my deep breathing inside myself to a quiet place. My energy shifts inward and I remember why I'm here. HP has hired me to serve. I'm here to serve. I don't let the customer's emotions become my emotions. Staying centered internally allows me to remain caring and gracious no matter how angry they become. It's also great for my blood pressure. [He laughs].

Vincent's story reminds us that the quality of our stopping also matters. As the late Indian Prime Minister Indira Gandhi once said, "You must learn to be still in the midst of activity and to be vibrantly alive in repose." In the midst of the madness we can literally or metaphorically stop, and, even as we continue our work, we can enter the quiet eye of the storm. From this centered perspective we can be in our work world but not of it. We can remain fully engaged, yet at the same time, be observant and transcendent.

Sometimes the invitation to stop comes as a persistent inner voice that urges us to take a break and put time and space between our work activities and ourselves. Few workers have the courage or the perceived resources to heed this call. So we sweep this yearning under the proverbial rug, hoping it will go away. But it doesn't, and many go an entire worklife dodging this urge for a sabbatical that will never materialize. Greg Levoy in his thoughtful book *Callings* teaches us that a call is a persistent question that doesn't go away until it is answered. Part of us says, "This makes no sense." But another part of us knows our life will make no sense if we fail to answer the call. Consider the following account of a young woman who works in a grueling political arena that often leads to burnout.

SARA MERZ'S STORY:
"Time Out!"

I started working in politics by accident. My first job out of college was working on a political campaign. I had no idea what I wanted to do with my life after college and because my parents and I had always been active in civic matters, working on a campaign made sense as something I cared about. One thing led to another and I ended up working for a fabulous state senator who holds self and others to the highest standards. It was an exciting opportunity to learn, grow, and serve in this arena with an incredibly astute and forward-looking leader.

But politics is a difficult and contradictory field. While I didn't have to put myself on the line in the same way the senator did, I had to deal with losses, disappointments, being opposed or undermined, and struggling to make policy changes against tremendous obstacles. Don't get me wrong; we had enormous successes too, with far reaching implications in important areas such as child protection and criminal justice. The highs were way high and the lows way low. I found myself having to deal with anger, loss, and feelings of victimhood or powerlessness, and to face huge struggles. I began feeling like I was in the wrong place.

At first I stayed out of not knowing what else to do. Gradually I was losing faith in my ability to make a difference in the political world. I knew I needed to do something to heal myself, so I went away for ten days on a meditation retreat. I returned to work. But things no longer worked for me. In the midst of the legislative session, I quit my job and went to Thailand, this time for six weeks on a second retreat. I returned to the U.S. feeling both peaceful and scared. I didn't have a clue what was in store for me.

Eventually, quite by accident, and quite ironically, I landed another job in politics. Part of me felt "this makes no sense," yet part of me felt "this is very right for me." Right now I'm doing more policy work than in my previous job. I'm having a different experience, not just because the job is different, but because I'm different. My meditation work taught me a lot about how to approach things. Stopping also gave me a chance to get perspective on things. I've learned to let go of extreme judgment when people see things differently from me. I now can disagree with people of a different party or with a view that opposes mine and still feel a sense of camaraderie and teamwork.

Today I work in a different political arena and I bring a different emotional mindset. It's been very liberating. I feel renewed and very hopeful as I face the future.

Working in politics is no easy challenge. Sara works in an arena that is much maligned and stereotyped in ways that give us little insight into the real experiences and the inner lives of its workers. Perhaps more than any other profession, politicians struggle with how to make peace with work that poses impossible polarities and dilemmas to manage.

Elected public officials and their support staff come from a range of backgrounds—farmers and physicians, lawyers and businesspeople, homemakers and educators, self-employed and employers of others. They come to their work with varying faiths, ethnic backgrounds, educational levels, and values. Some are retirees bringing long years of leadership experience. Others are young parents juggling work and family along with their civic duties.

Most are hoping to do something extraordinary for the constituents they represent. Most bring high hopes and high ideals to the leadership positions that guide and inform our democracy. But, as elected officials, there is always this trap: Once in office they face a "crisis of meaning" as their values and vision butt up against harsh political realities.

Like workers in every sector, they must juggle competing demands, manage time crunches, and get desired results. They must also digest monumental amounts of information in order to understand and guide the direction of public policy. And they must be equally adept at breaking down resistance to change and at building new alliances across diverse constituents and stakeholders.

In addition, the madness of their work world carries some unique challenges. Invariably these public servants face the love-hate ambivalence of constituents and the media who simultaneously cast them as bearers of hope and egotistical power mongers. Walking this tightrope of public scrutiny requires vigilance, courage, and a fierce commitment to purpose. When they succeed, supporters laud them. If they fail, this confirms the bias of those ready to pounce on the frailties of political leaders or vote them out of office.

The work life of those in politics is also marked by multiple crises that compete for their attention. But the most difficult crisis they ultimately face is an inner one, associated with gut wrenching questions such as: Shall I speak my truth and risk losing votes, or tow the line so I can continue to serve? How will I reconcile the demands of the "machinery" with my own basic values? What compromises am I willing to make to achieve the goals before me? How can I represent the conflicting needs of diverse constituents and be true to my own values, passion, and purpose?

Such dilemmas, while troublesome, can also be useful. There is a sense in which we all wrestle with such crises of integrity: When to speak up and when to be silent? How to be true to our organizations and to ourselves? If we address and manage them by stopping for deep reflection, these work-related dilemmas can become catalysts for personal growth and development of leadership skills as we learn to bring our inner and outer worlds into greater alignment. But this always involves risk, and risk-taking can be costly. For the politician, it may mean the difference between continuing to serve and being voted out of office. As an elected official in one of my seminars put it, "I find myself wondering how much of me am I prepared to give up in order to continue to serve."

There are no easy answers for such dilemmas for politicians or for the rest of us. Not everyone can afford the luxury of a sabbatical. Few are brave enough, as Sara was, to risk it anyway. But one thing is for sure: We must make time to stop in order to journey inward, to get clear about where we stand and what we stand for. By embracing this inner work, we will have an easier time negotiating the moral mazes and political quandaries that are an inevitable part of working in any sector.

One of the gifts of my personal crisis of meaning is I have begun to experiment with other ways of stopping at work. As a writer, I regularly stop to silence the critic on my shoulder. Going inward, I pray for guidance, and listen. This gives me access to a deeper knowing, the part of me that's free from judgment or fear. I now carry this practice into my work as a lecturer. I consciously stop after posing a question. I literally count to twenty, allowing participants to pause to gather their thoughts or to ponder an idea just shared by another. I am aware of the potency of the space between the notes of dialogue. At first, it creates a good deal of anxiety for seminar participants who have not yet learned to be comfortable with stopping. So these days, I've begun to teach people the power of stopping. Instead of rushing in with a quick answer, I encourage them to pause, go inward, and reflect in the twenty-second space I have created. To the reader twenty seconds may not seem like much time, but it feels like eons to audiences who are just not used to stopping to reflect in classrooms or meetings.

> "You must learn to be still in the midst of activity and to be vibrantly alive in repose."
>
> —INDIRA GANDHI

Perhaps the greatest gift of learning to stop to reflect on our work is that the practice begins to spill over to other aspects of living. We stop to watch children at play and recapture lost pieces of our own childhood. We return to a place of awe and joyfulness, and if we are mindful, we can bring this awareness into our work. We pause to give thanks or ask for Guidance before darting into the next workday task, and our activities are elevated to a more potent level. Creativity happens. We get to savor the emotional rewards of a job well done.

We ask a friend how she is doing and *really stop* to listen and connect in ways that are life affirming for both parties. We discover that stopping to make time for the people and things we care about outside of work makes us more whole, because we come to know ourselves more fully in relationships with others. We deepen our creativity and broaden our perspectives through pastimes, leisure activities, and friendships.

This applies at work as well. Stopping for laughter or to compare experiences, share our struggles, learn from each other, and get support from colleagues is undoubtedly key to making peace at work. Stopping to relate renews us, enhances our work climate, and makes us better prepared to reengage with our work in a more meaningful way.

Stopping in nature is also useful. The best teachers on the subject of work life transformation draw on nature as a source of information about organizational dynamics and about life in general. Nature teaches us the power and importance of living in harmony. Wind and water, earth and fire, and all of the rich minerals and resources of Mother Earth combine to create the world as we know it. Together they form a complex, yet elegantly simple, web of interconnections needed to sustain life as we know it. Into this space we bring our humanity. And in our earnest attempts to sustain and propagate ourselves, we build families, establish communities, and arrange ourselves into organizations to do the work of our lives. At their very best, these organizations mirror nature. At their worst, they threaten to destroy nature and humanity with it.

Lucky for us, nature is a willing teacher. She contains and reveals the codes for our survival. We can access this information to assist us in any transformation, if we are willing to stop and take note.

Perhaps in our work we can be like trees: anchored in the present, yielding in the storm, changing with the seasons, willingly giving up the fruits of our labor to nourish and sustain humanity. I often use the sun and sea to fire my passions and soothe my soul. Whether I am composing a book, a workshop or my life anew, or stopping to fuel myself after months of intense activity, I find it useful to return to my native Jamaica where I stop, get rooted once more, and tap into the energy of sun and sea to revitalize my work.

The exercise that follows invites you to practice stopping as a path to renewal.

INVITATION
Practice Stopping to Renew
Yourself and Your Work

Consider this excerpt from the opening of this chapter:

Make a conscious effort to balance stopping with going and to find new ways to think about time in and time out. For example, instead of only taking sick days off, you might benefit from taking a well day off once in a while, or you could make a project out of stopping periodically to redis-cover the lost aspects of your work or to rethink how you are working.

In your journal explore:

1. If you took a sabbatical off from work for a year, what would you do?
   What might you discover?
2. What do you need to stop, or let go of, in order to create space to reflect and renew yourself and your work?

SEVEN

When Life Interrupts

Sometimes we don't consciously initiate the necessary stopping. Instead, life stops us in our tracks, interrupting our careers or whatever else we had planned. Two-thirds of the way through the writing of this book, my writing came to a screeching halt. My mother had become seriously ill, and my thoughts and every spare moment were consumed with her care and concern for her well-being. Writer's block set in, and I watched with dismay as publishing deadlines came and went. The focus of my workday shifted from career to family, and my writing project slipped further and further away. The amazing thing was that the title of the book stayed with me as a mantra playing through my head all the time in a way that said pay attention to the meaning behind the message: *Making Peace with Your Work*. I prayed about my dilemma—how to be fully present for both family care and my commitment to my work in the larger world.

The answer quickly and clearly: *Life is calling you to attend to your inner work—to reconcile the work of your career with the currently more pressing work within your family system.* This awareness freed me to let go of the writing project, confident that this book would re-emerge in time, enhanced by my experience of care giving. I now fully understand what my poetry teacher meant when she reminded us, "whatever you work at becomes your work."

We must pay attention to the meaning in the work that engages us inside or outside of our place of employment. Often what feels like being pulled off track is simply new, more important work wanting to happen through us. In this respect, the aspect of our work that is our job or career—that pays the bills—often does battle with our larger work.

We are called to wrestle with, and learn from, a crisis of meaning whenever our work is interrupted by a harrowing life event. Our company goes belly up, and suddenly we are unemployed. We lose our most important customer to the competition. We come to our senses one day and think, "What am I doing here? I hate this job." A sudden illness knocks us off our feet, and we are challenged to fight our way back to health. These occurrences, while painful at the time, are also calls to action. They signal us to pay attention to other, perhaps larger, work—perhaps talent wanting to shine through or our hearts opening to the loving care of self or another. Here is the inspiring story of how one woman rose to meet the challenge of being stopped.

DR. M. FRANCES BALDWIN'S STORY:
"Healing From The Inside Out"

"I was having a good life, doing consulting work both internally and externally for major corporations. I lived and worked internationally, enjoying the work that was, in fact, shaping and engulfing my entire life. Suddenly my illness hit. I went from fully functioning to being diagnosed with arthritis and unable to get myself out of bed without considerable effort. It was like falling off a cliff. I'd always taken very good care of my body—and had had no chronic illnesses. Suddenly I was in excruciating pain and unable to work. This was shocking—like the screeching halt of a fast-moving train. I felt broken, out of my element, life context, and experience.

I was humbled. I needed my physicians, and I listened desperately turning to them as my first resource. But I soon decided that, as skilled as they were, they had limitations. Their prognosis was invariably negative. One doctor said, "You will get worse at an accelerated rate because that is the nature of this disease."

Shocked and alarmed, I decided that I had to do something on a scale equal to the trauma I was experiencing. The day I decided to choose healing, I flung myself into the wall before me and discovered that it was not the permanent wall I feared, but something permeable. I decided to move to the other side of the wall and the Universe conspired with me. People appeared who literally brought each piece of the puzzle precisely when I needed it. I found a doctor who is truly advanced in his practice and highly regarded in his field and whose approach was to control the disease. Alternative healers came to assist as well, engaging me in fasting and deep bodywork.

The thread weaving throughout this experience was my spirituality. I learned that the source of my health would not be the tactical, physical, scientific interventions—medicines, heating pads, and the like. My healing had to be a process that came from the inside out. My journey was spiritual in the broadest sense. It included art, poetry, music, values, knowing, faith, the sacred, the Divine. I brought my current self to my religious roots. I discovered that I had been a consumer of religion, not an active participant in its spiritual aspects. Today I am pain-free, agile, and energetic. This life crisis has had a cleansing effect and brought me to a deeper, richer place. I let go of the arthritis because I no longer needed it. It did its work, and I chose to do my work in relation to it.

Now everything about me works better. Things are still emerging. I am now very much attached to the purpose of my work—who I'm trying to help to do what. I'm less interested in helping profit-motivated enterprises and more committed to helping organizations that are working for the greater good. The Universe continues to conspire to assist me.

Crisis puts us in touch with the work—the real work—we need to do at any given moment in our lives. It is not so much an interruption of whatever else we were doing, but a call to go deeper and connect with our wisdom. Frances' decision to *choose* healing was transformative. It allowed her to call into play all of her inner resources and to join forces with others who show up to work with us in times of great change. Her story also reminds us that the work we do, whether to heal ourselves or to heal the world, is done in community.

INVITATION
See the Opportunities
Behind Interruptions

Some interruptions are unwanted time wasters. The colleague who pops in and out of your workspace to chit chat when you have made it clear you're working against a pressing deadline is one such example.

But sometimes an interruption is nature's way of inviting us to stop and attend to something more pressing or more important in our lives.

In your journal explore the following:

1. What unexpected interruption have you experienced in your work or life recently?
2. How has it served you?
3. What has it taught you?

EIGHT

When Work
No Longer Works

When we join the workforce, we marry our personal hopes and dreams to those of the organization. If the relationship is compatible, both parties are mutually satisfied. We make a good living, and the organization achieves it goals or is profitable. Our work enhances our lives and the lives of those we serve. We are able to balance time in with time out to rejuvenate ourselves. Workplace policy and practices are family friendly, and we have easy access to the education, training, and mentoring we need to do our best work. There is a fairly good match between our personal and organizational values, and we often feel empowered to influence the things over which we have control.

When difficulties arise, we get the support and resources we need to work things through to satisfaction. We are able to face the madness headlong, energized by a sense of purpose and possibilities. We see setbacks as temporary challenges that take us out of our comfort zones and into our learning zones. This way we are enriched by changes for the better. Rather than losing hope, we remain creative and committed. Most days we are satisfied with the financial, emotional, and spiritual rewards of our work, and the organization is satisfied with our contribution.

OUR IDEALIZED WORKPLACE

Earlier I mentioned the ideal self—the part of us that approaches perfection. Somewhere in the backs of our minds, we carry a picture of the ideal workplace as well. It is a place of service and community that warms the heart. Worker and customer, employer and employee collaborate, create, and have fun in the exchange. This ideal workplace provides a sense of potency and belonging for employees whose work is appreciated and fairly compensated. It is a place of personal growth, a place of creativity, and it offers freedom and security, respite, and challenge. In the ideal, we honor our workplace because it sustains us and our families, as we offer up our time and talents. The workplace, in turn, honors us for our contributions.

Sometimes, captivated by our hope for this ideal, we persist in a particular occupation or bad situation long after the cries of our inner self have risen to a crescendo. Our motivation wanes, we dread Monday mornings, and waves of nausea hit us when the elevator door to our workplace closes us in, yet we continue to hang on. We continue because we are taught to silence our inner knowing. We have learned to ignore the cues of our bodies, our minds, and our spirit at work.

We may listen instead to the good opinion of others who try to convince us that we have it made. Or we may be held spellbound by fears, so we persist in work that no longer works for us. Every day I meet people who are secretly planning their getaway from a job that, decades earlier, was to be a temporary way station after leaving school. Some have been scheming or talking about how awful things are and how ready they are to leave for years. They are trapped—locked into a codependent relationship with an employer. Leaving becomes an increasingly elusive option, so they stay with clenched fists and gritted teeth until the bitter end. "Forty years in the same job, and I hated every moment of it."

When we languish in work that has lost its significance for us, we find ourselves at war with our work. Our souls crave more meaning but our daily grind puts us at odds with our deepest desires. When a work pursuit no longer works for us emotionally, we must turn inward posing the question, "Does my soul crave stopping?" We must listen to our guts. The story that follows is an example of how the soul of the worker can assert itself through physical, visceral cues.

ROBIN GETMAN'S STORY:
"Soul Food"

I felt drawn to acting and went to school to be an actress, earning a degree in theatre. But once on stage, things went wrong. I felt ill backstage every time, gripped by stage fright. I worried about forgetting lines; I got butterflies in my stomach, but I persisted telling myself that it's normal to have stage fright—after all Meryl Streep and Barbra Streisand do.

Eventually it was too much to bear. I left theatre and took paying jobs—waiting tables. At tableside, customers laughed at everything I said. I was, in a sense, back in theatre, but this time without the stage fright. The restaurant manager noticed and said, "Will you be a trainer for the corporation? You're so good with people." So I moved up into training and was great at it. That's when it became clear to me. No matter what, I just have to have an audience. My soul craves this.

Along the way, they gave me increasing responsibility. I was promoted all the way up [out of training] to general manager, but eventually left to start my own training company. Training was in my blood. It just fed my soul. I couldn't let go of it.

My former boss at the restaurant got me an audience, The Upper Midwest Hospitality Show. I did a skit showing examples of good and bad service, and then engaged the audience in dialogue about customer service. At the end, managers and restaurant owners came down the aisle to get my business card. My new business, Skits At Your Service, was born. For three years I toured and did customer service skits for clients like the Hyatt and other hotels and resorts.

Again, I tried to go back on stage. This time I took a stand-up comedy class and tried stand-up comedy. It was scarier than acting. I got the same message: The one place I feel most at home is the speaking and training field. It's the one place where I don't get physically ill.

I learned that I could bring aspects of comedy and acting into my speaking and training business. But I must remain true to what my soul wants. It's all about giving myself permission to be all of me and to do what I enjoy and feel comfortable doing.

Now I'm intrigued with questions like, How do I bring my whole self to work? How do I follow my gut in choosing what I do? How do leaders give permission for people to show up as whole persons? How do employees show respect for organizational constraints, so both parties can find and do what's appropriate, so that when I, as an employee, do what moves me forward, that doesn't detract from the organization's mission?

Listening to her gut, Robin has learned to move away from the ego's pull to be an actor or the organization's attempts to seduce her into management. She feeds her soul—her deep love of training—by using the pleasure principle (What feels good? What feels right? What makes my heart sing?) to guide her toward right choices. She reminds us that at times there are *aspects* of a large body of work that aren't right for us. But in making peace, we needn't discard the whole thing. We might simply need to transform how we work.

Work, like life, is a developmental process. As babies we start out totally dependent on others for our survival. This is also how we first enter the work world. We then embarked on a life-long process of growth towards being self-sustaining or independent. We learn as babies to roll from side to side, to sit, to crawl on all fours, and to pull ourselves up. Next, standing on sea legs, we toddle painstakingly, conscientiously, with the help of those who pick up us and cheer us on. Most of us finally learn to walk on our own. In the process we learn that before we can be independent, we must first learn interdependence. We learn we can be an apprentice to life. Parents, bosses, peers, teachers, and others have a role to play in this learning process. This movement from reliance on another, to interdependence, and, where appropriate, independence is a metaphor that runs consistent through work and life, in our relationships with family, organizations, and our larger community.

But there is always the danger that we can get stuck in a form of dependency that becomes sustained helplessness. There is also the danger of forming codependent relationships with our organization.

We have the power to choose how we come to terms with our work. Regardless of the type of work we do, or the condition surrounding our work, we can transform it into an enriching adventure by transforming ourselves. We can then connect with the higher purpose behind our work, take work that is already satisfying, and deepen our experience of it, or, if our work no longer works, we can make peace with it, even as we plan an exit.

MAKING PEACE AS YOU LEAVE

When I decided to downshift to a simpler lifestyle, my first step was to sell my six-bedroom home and find a smaller, maintenance-free condominium. I knew I had made the right decision, but I was overcome by sadness. I couldn't shake the sense of loss. It wasn't my favorite house. My decision to sell was very sound financially, so was my decision to downsize to something less taxing and more affordable. I had never had problems with leave-taking before. Compared to most people I have changed my place of residence often, sometimes even on a whim. Always I had relished the newness and the untapped creativity that come with new beginnings. But not this time.

Wanting to understand these feelings, I asked for guidance. As I wandered about the house listening, the answer came clearly. I had been so focused on the challenges of this house, which I'd begun to call the money pit, that I'd lost touch with the joy it also brought me over the years I'd lived there. I had some unfinished business with the house. My sadness was a cue that I needed to fully experience and honor the house before I could leave.

For a whole month before leaving, I made peace with the home. I tended it carefully and lovingly, savored the view, which was, in fact, the finest I'd ever been blessed with up to that point. I carefully painted and carried out cosmetic repairs for the new owners. I thoughtfully put together a file with all the special things about the home and included a directory of service people who had done installations or repairs in case my out-of-town buyers needed such references. I made a ritual of visiting each room and reminiscing about the special activities and guests that had graced the room. My feelings of sadness were replaced by pure gratitude. I begin to see lovely features of the home that I'd completely overlooked.

Preparing to leave in this more conscious way was spiritually uplifting and fun for me. Most importantly, I discovered that by connecting with the joy of having lived in this particular home, I freed myself to travel more lightly.

In coaching employees who are ready to move on, I notice the same scenario playing out. They decide to leave but begin to second guess the decision. They are ready to go but feel a sense of foreboding or a deep loss. With any ending it's appropriate to feel sadness, but when you can't shake the sadness it may be an invitation to make peace—to heal your relationship with your present job, because as the saying goes, "wherever you go, there you are."

If you are thinking of moving on, consider the following. Are there any projects on the back burner that, if completed before you leave, would bring you deep satisfaction? Is there something you need to say to someone, a relationship you need to repair? What legacy do you want to leave behind? Is there a way to package and share what you know so your successor's load can be made lighter? Most importantly, take stock of the lessons learned. No job is ever wasted. What insights, skills, competencies, and wisdom will you take as you move on? And how will you deploy these?

Retiring From or Retiring To?

Many people see retirement as a (hopefully long) vacation from working for a living. For some, this means being willing to spend their best years of life engaged in work they may or may not find fulfilling, so that in their latter years of life they can enjoy the break they finally get. What if they finally retire, only to find that their body, battered and bruised by hard work, no longer works?

Here is the story of a boomer couple who chose to rethink their work—and their lives—in the process.

MYRNA AND TIMOTHY BULLOCK'S STORY:
"Answering The Call To Reinvent Our Life's Work"

As we entered mid-life and the celebration of twenty-five years together as a couple, we decided it was time to transcend our fears, leave our traditional jobs, and pursue a passion we both felt strongly about—a life of service on the African continent. This had been an early dream for both of us. Myrna wanted to live and work in Africa since she was fifteen years old. Timothy planned, with a childhood friend at age nine, to stow-away on a vessel, a cargo ship headed to Africa.

What we envisioned was integrating our lives, love, and work into a cohesive whole, spending our waking and sleeping hours together, traveling, helping others, making our own decisions about how our time is spent in this life. We had grown tired of the separations created by the "live to work" reality we experienced in America. We dreamed of a "freedom to live" lifestyle, which allowed us to be open to and moved by the flow of Spirit working in and through us in a conscious way.

The challenge for us was not only in moving forward, but also in detaching from the past. How do you move away from the perceived security of a way of life that has always sustained you? How do you convince yourself, and your loved ones, that moving away from the accepted norms of modern living is not just a flight of fancy, but a well-thought-out plan to change our way of thinking and being?

We took our initial leap of faith when we joined the Interfaith Pilgrimage of the Middle Passage in 1998. The initial Pilgrimage was a year-long walk that retraced the route and the history of the Atlantic slave trade (from North America to the Caribbean to South America to West Africa) that positioned us to confront and to explore the horrific events of the enslavement of African people in the Americas, to grieve our lost ancestors, and to locate ourselves in the continuum of African history and tradition. We divested ourselves of all of our worldly possessions—house and home, furnishings, and all of our "stuff" in order to be free to live the Pilgrimage and not be tied down by belongings and debts.

Participation in the Middle Passage Pilgrimage introduced us to spiritual pilgrimage as a means to social change, self-discovery, and healing. It has left us poised and ready to live and work differently in the world. We have walked many places in the world to "work" since 1998—fifteen different countries in three continents.

We have also found ourselves, our real selves, rich with gifts and talents, resources, courage, faith, and love enough to sustain us through the trials and battles of our chosen life, and compassionate enough for us to share with others. It was impossible to return to our old narrow, though interesting and busy, lives in the United States after having tasted the global life.

In the year 2000, we founded a grassroots peace and social justice ministry, SpiritWalkers, which promotes healing and transformation by creating spiritual solutions to our global concerns as the platform for us to offer our God-given gifts in our global community. We currently live in Gege, Swaziland, a rural community in southeastern Africa, where we work to build a community resource center that addresses the education and prevention, care and support, for those stricken with HIV/AIDS and other life-threatening situations.

We have come to believe that a job is something that you do for someone else, so they don't have to do it themselves. But work is something that we each must do for ourselves, whether we earn money in the process or not. Success is not the accumulation of riches, but is the outcome of a commitment of time, effort, gifts, and talents into anything that benefits us and the wider community for the common or higher good. So, giving of our time and energy to a social concern or cause, to work for something we believe in, is a valid and very spiritual way to operate in the world.

For us, success is no longer measured by money or status, but is realized in each and every moment as we continue to be fully committed to our life's work.

In 2006, the oldest baby boomers turn sixty. For most of this generation, retirement is fraught with ambivalence. Ask any boomer about their plans for retirement and you are likely to get a wish list of activities, careers, and entrepreneurial ventures that make your head spin. Partly, we boomers are driven by a healthy, and sometimes not so healthy, preoccupation with work. As a generation, boomers epitomized the drive for material success, which often led to workaholism. Boomers are also motivated by a realistic concern that in an age of longevity and consumerist lifestyles, their money pits aren't deep enough to see them through the forty-plus years of retirement they secretly hope for.

So there is an emerging trend that says we aren't retiring *from* work, but retiring *to* involve ourselves in new livelihoods and new ways of being in the world. Now, as a boomer, this actually excites me. But it also begs the question, *why wait?*

Instead of waiting, respond to the invitation that follows and discover new directions for your future.

INVITATION
Be Willing To Strike Out
in New Directions

Retiring at age sixty-something from a life-long job with a nice gold watch may fire some people's engine, but these days most workers are open to a range of other options. In fact, Cliff Hakim said it best when he wrote the timely book, *We Are All Self-Employed.* Hakim advises us to adopt a new attitude—a self-employed outlook—in today's unstable work world. Instead of seeing ourselves as working for an organization, he suggests we see ourselves as working with the organization—for as long as the partnership works for both parties. Instead of waiting for an employer to pull the rug out from under us, we should be ever aware of our needs, our worth, and our options so we can be personally more powerful—choosing how we work, where we work, and for how long.

What excites me most about approaching work this way is that it positions us to discover our purpose and passion so we can orient ourselves in a direction that is most satisfying for us.

In your journal explore the following:

1. What do you want from your work?
2. What do you have to offer? If, as the poet-philosopher, Gibran, says, "work is love made visible," how is love made visible through your work?

3. How would your workplace, your profes-
    sion, or the world be different if
    you had not be born?

4. What aspect of your work no longer
    works? How can you tell?

5. What are your options outside of your
    present occupation? What are your
    unexplored options inside of your present
    occupation?

NINE

The Hagberg Model:
Six Stages of
Personal Power At Work

We tend to equate the word power with achievement in the external world. "He's at the top of his game," we say, meaning the executive has authority, influence, organizational clout, and leadership prowess. "My coworker is power-hungry," we complain, of someone who imposes his or her will through coercion, manipulation, or abuse. Power often strikes fear in our hearts because it is—well, powerful.

Yet, to make peace with our work, we must learn to make peace with power. Workplaces, like life, leadership, and liberty, are fueled by power—the capacity to achieve desired outcomes.

Chances are good that wherever you work there is talk of the organization's vision, mission, goals, objectives, strategies, priorities, action plans, and the measures and metrics that define and direct these pursuits. All of this hinges on organizational power. A vision gives us a North Star to which we can fix our gaze if we are to remain true to the mission before us. Goals attained are a measure of our mastery and our financial worth in the external world. Leaders and managers rise and fall in direct relationship to their ability to strategize and to get people mobilized in the right direction with the right resources and skills for high achievement. Competent supervisors and the workers that report to them must not only achieve goals; these days they must exceed customers' expectations. Without such discipline—such power to make things happen—organizations falter and fail.

Most workers at some point in their lives are also motivated towards this power to achieve. We hope, in the jargon of organizational life, to be *em*powered so we can achieve more success. As a result, we seek the guidance, expertise, credentials, position, money, and authority needed to make things happen. In fact, one of the reasons people resist change is that change carries with it a temporary loss of competence, and therefore of our sense of power. Even when we embrace change, we may hesitate, paralyzed momentarily by our fears of being disempowered. We resist being snatched out of a comfort zone where we know which goals to pursue, what to do, and how to do it well.

INNER POWER—THE HAGBERG MODEL

However, the power to exert influence in the external world is only one-half of the equation. Real power—the personal power needed to create our own work life experience in the outer world—comes from doing inner work.

This awareness has been the greatest gift I received on my journey to *Making Peace with My Work*. It comes from the groundbreaking work of my friend and colleague Janet O. Hagberg who has generously given me permission to include her Real Power model in this book. In her book *Real Power: Stages of Personal In Organizations,* Hagberg describes personal power as a developmental journey from powerlessness to wisdom. Over the course of this journey we grow from being externally focused on expertise, titles, status, and material concerns to include an internal focus marked by deep introspection, integration of the lessons of personal struggles, self-acceptance, and a sense of purpose. If we are to truly make peace with our work, we must go beyond the traditional constraints of organizational power to become personally powerful. Only then can we be the creative authors of our work life stories.

Hagberg defines personal power as "the extent to which one is able to link the outer capacity for action (external power) with the inner capacity for reflection (internal power)." By this definition, some people in influential positions in organizations are not *personally* powerful. Conversely, some people have very little organizational power, but they have an inner, reflective life that allows them to be personally more powerful. Through reflection and transcendence they tap their inner resources. They are guided by clarity of purpose and are willing to be *other than who the world wants them to be.*

The following generalizations will help you to understand these stages.

1. The stages are developmental. This means they are experienced in sequence. You can only grow to the next stage by resolving the developmental struggles of the stage you are in.

2. At any stage you can feel satisfied. At any stage you can feel stuck.

3. You can stay at the same stage for a lifetime. Or you may feel compelled to keep learning as much as possible and to find ways to keep moving.

4. Power is experienced differently at each stage.

5. It is easier to understand the stage you're in than the stages beyond yours.

6. You do not necessarily proceed to the next stage with age or experience, although both are factors. Movement from one stage to another is usually precipitated by a personal crisis.

7. Stages 1-3 are linked more closely with external power. Stages 4-6 are linked to internal power.

8. The stages of power are complex. You can be in different stages of power in different areas of your life, at different times, and with different people.

STAGE 1. POWERLESSNESS

As adults, if this is our home stage, we feel powerless because we think there is nothing we can do that will make any difference in our lives. We are dependent on other people, and we think we need to get our needs met through them by being submissive. We may feel secure, but usually it is at a dear price, even if we aren't aware of it. Or we feel trapped, frequently angry, and powerless to change the forces that surround us. In organizations we have very little knowledge or information and believe we wouldn't know what to do with it, even if we got more of it.

When we get stuck in this stage, we act out our powerlessness by being victims of others' behaviors. We are like doormats, "inviting" people to walk on us. Martyrs are also stuck at Stage One. To move out of this stage we need to develop self-esteem and learn new skills that allow us to acknowledge our potential and take responsibility for ourselves.

STAGE 2. POWER BY ASSOCIATION

At Stage Two we are apprentices to power. We are learners, absorbing all we can about how to do the right things and do them well in order to be successful. We seek out mentors. We follow others' behavior. We are enthusiastic and eager. Although we know what power is and who has it, we don't have it yet ourselves. We are in the learning process. And it is all right to make mistakes.

Each time we recycle from one job to another, we re-experience the apprentice stage in the new environment, learning the ropes all over again. It is a wonderful stage to experience if we know our development needs and our boss gives us opportunities for growth. But it is also the stage in which women get stuck the most. If we want to develop and mature in our power, we must gain confidence to deal with the issue of control—whether dealing with self or others.

Often we get stuck at this trying to be "good" or like someone else in order to be accepted or to avoid conflict. And to move to the next stage, we need to develop self-confidence and release the high need for security, or affirmation, from others.

STAGE 3. POWER BY ACHIEVEMENT

This is the stage where we feel we've arrived. We have power, and we may even feel successful. We see results. It is exhilarating and, at times, very stressful. This stage rewards hard work, setting and meeting goals, planning, and confidence. We have more self-confidence, we are knowledgeable in our area of specialty, and we focus on positive attitudes and challenges. Leadership positions are what we relish. In a word, achievement of all kinds is our by-word. We can deal with conflict and can challenge others on a professional level. And we like as much control in our lives as possible.

In the introduction to this book, I mention being seen by others as successful, yet not *feeling* successful. Hagberg's description of Stage Three allowed me to do two things. First, to appreciate that this is a necessary stage on the path to personal power, for it allows us to flex our success muscles in the traditional, cultural sense of the word. Living at Stage Three is nothing to be ashamed of. It prepares us for what's to come. It allows us to sharpen our saw of expertise, confidence, risk-taking, and winning competence.

Second, in describing Stage Three, Hagberg reminds us that it is easy to get stuck at this stage. It is very seductive and exhilarating. However, if we continue to grow personally and professionally, we may come to a place where we begin to question, "Is this all there is?" We begin to feel something is still lacking. We begin to experience dissonance between what we are feeling on the inside and how we are living in our outer worlds. This is an invitation to move to Stage Four, and to begin to reflect more deeply on our *values, priorities,* and *direction* in life.

MY PERSONAL STORY:
"A Crisis of Meaning"

My mother, well into her eighties and retired, continued to set goals and make daily to-do lists. Her commitment to work fed her self-esteem and kept her vibrantly alive for many years. Outside of the classroom she was private and reserved. She dabbled in crafts, wrote in her diaries, and perused books and magazines for hours in search of new information for her students. In her classroom she sprang alive. Her exuberance, her timing, her devotion, and her knack for bringing learning to life was—well, magical. And in the forty-odd years she spent preparing students for life, she never doubted that her work was a very special calling. Teaching was her first love. Teaching was her life.

I inherited my mother's devotion to right livelihood, although in my undergrad years I rebelled against her career choice. I majored in psychology, briefly switched to biology, and then considered economics. I finally settled on speech pathology. My goal was to veer far away from the schoolteacher's calling that so defined my mother. Perhaps it was because growing up I competed with term papers and grade books for mother's time. Or it could have been simply what psychologists call individuation. In the end, her parental inspiration won out. I had tried to choose otherwise, but the field of education chose me. I surrendered, earned a Doctor of Education degree at Columbia University, and embraced my career with a passion and purpose equal to hers.

It is no coincidence that I should attempt to write a book about work. I am part of a family system whose core values center on education and hard work. In fact, my earliest childhood memories are of mimicking my parents' work. I would sit watching mother write lesson plans and grade student papers while father sorted through health department documents at his huge oak desk. In my make-believe office I would craft imaginary lesson plans and shuffle and stamp my own documents gleefully. I remember the mixed emotions of excitement and dread when my father, a department of health meat inspector, received menacing threats from farmers after he condemned their contaminated meat. I marveled at the power my father wielded in his work and wondered whether my own work would command equal attention when I grew up.

So, not surprisingly, I have made a pastime and a very successful career out of observing and coaching workers.

This calling has taken me from work as a professor of management, to work as a corporate human resources professional, and finally to work as organizational development consultant, writer, lecturer, and executive coach. Now I spend my days supporting people at every organizational level in their quest to heal their organizations and their work lives.

Like my clients, my work life has had its ups and downs. I have lived as though work was all that matters, and I have lived it as though it were a noose around my neck. Luckily, most of the time I have enjoyed work that is deeply satisfying and enjoyable, but there have also been brief periods where I have had to do unsatisfying jobs to get by. I have built a successful small business and gone through the pain and exhilaration of moving on to something else.

Fresh out of high school, I hired into a safe job to work my way through college, only to find myself disoriented, "dissed," and eventually displaced by the elimination of my department. Later I landed a position I really loved, only to have my creative ideas silenced by workplace politics and fear-based management. I have worked on high performing teams where I was so enthused I couldn't wait to get up and return to work the next day. I have worked in situations where my aspirations were at odds with my employers', and I have had the good fortune as a young assistant professor at Brooklyn College, City University of New York, to be hired and coached for high performance by an employer whose confidence in my potential outstripped my own.

In 1980, I joined the graduate management faculty of Carnegie Mellon University and found a nurturing work environment where my research and teaching in management and organizational effectiveness flourished. From there new doors opened, introducing me into the world of business, government, and nonprofit consulting. By age forty I had built a reputable consulting practice, continued to teach as an adjunct faculty, and served on numerous boards. I was doing exactly what I love to do, and I was blessed with loyal clients, eager students, and smart, supportive colleagues and mentors who showered me with accolades and gave me enormous opportunities to learn and grow. I worked hard, put in long hours, devoted all my spare time and energy to parenting my son, took vacations in exotic places, and was generally sailing along feeling successful.

So imagine my surprise when, without warning, my inner compass shifted. On the surface I bobbed along perfectly—committed to my clients and students, practicing my craft well. But underneath I found myself paddling furiously to stay afloat. "I love my work!" I asserted, trying to silence the question marks that were beginning to surface. "So why do I feel like something is missing?" my better judgment asked. "What I do is useful to those who hire me," I reasoned. "Surely that should be enough."

But it no longer was. And this made no sense at first. Unknown to me at the time, I was caught in the undercurrents of a predictable work life crisis—a crisis of meaning.

A crisis of meaning occurs when our inner world is no longer in alignment with our outer world. We can coast along for long periods of time—perhaps an entire lifetime—unaware of this misalignment. But once we become aware of it, it shocks us into reckoning with ourselves.

My crisis of meaning jarred me out of my denial, like the bearer of bad news who calls late at night. My first response was, surely you have the wrong number. But the caller persisted whispering urgently into my ear, "Pay attention. Something is amiss. What are you doing here? You're on seven boards, and you can't make time for your ailing elders."

For months this "Inner Caller" prodded and pried, refusing to go away until I gave her full attention. She insinuated herself into my psyche, throwing me off balance with her questions. She pulled me along a path of reflection forcing me to look deeper inside myself. She was at once provocateur and wise guide—posing tough questions and pointing to new possibilities. Turning inward, I came face to face with the lies I told myself. I was not just a devoted educator and organizational consultant. I had become a workaholic whose work and life were on a collision course. I had to face some hard truths about myself. Falling asleep at the office is not a sign of devotion. It's a sign of being out of control.

I later learned that I was not alone in this experience. Sooner or later (and especially as we leave Stage Three), we experience a crisis of meaning—a call to dig deeper and either reinvent our work experience or reconnect with our existing work in a more significant way.

STAGE 4. POWER BY REFLECTION

At this stage we go inside to rediscover who we are and how we can truly be that in our lives and work. We ask difficult questions about integrity and purpose like, "Why did I do that?" or "Why am I here anyway?" We emerge from that difficult task more clear about our chosen area of work, more collaborative, grounded in our uniqueness, and as wise mentors and conscious risk-takers. We operate on a set of inner principles that allows for the growth and support of others because we have less to lose and our security comes from inside ourselves. We can also put jobs or security on the line for a larger principle. We begin giving up control.

It is normal to experience intense personal confusion at this stage, or to feel grossly misunderstood. To move to the next stage we must give up our egos and experience the excruciatingly wonderful WALL between this stage and the next. But this is no easy task. The wall confronts us with our unloved qualities and compels us to face our selves—warts and all. As difficult as the wall is, it is also an inviting opportunity to let go. People can live very satisfying lives even if they never go through the wall. But going through it and learning the wisdom it has to teach us is life-changing. This is how Janet Hagberg describes the wall:

> The wall is a place of transformation. Once having experienced the wall, you will never be the same again. The wall is a place of tremendous loss and tremendous gain. It is exhilarating and it is painful. It is never easy. The wall is the place we face our inner selves, the truth of who we are, our shame, and ultimately our heart's deepest desires. We embrace all of this and learn to accept it. People describe the process of moving through the wall in these other ways: as a deep well, an abyss, a slow descent, a dark tunnel, a pit, a prison

*cell, a dark night. It is never pretty. But in it are
glimpses of wisdom and light. And it is healing, at a
deep level, a soul level.*

The wall is the place where we must lay our egos down
if we are to begin to move through to the other side. That
is a difficult and humbling process. Our egos serve us well,
for ego is linked to our basic drive to fight for survival—to
defend ourselves against powerlessness in the world and at
work. In contemporary life, this drive takes us beyond a
desire to fulfill basic needs. It compels us to succeed—to
grow, to thrive, to achieve more and more, faster and faster.
Our egos convince us that we are right, that we are capable,
and that we're "looking good!" as we enlist in our workplaces, captivated by the symbols of success—status, credentials, authority, money, and material comforts. Our egos
buoy us up as we aspire to make a good living and serve in
whatever capacity we chose or are chosen for. The ego,
though much maligned, is not all bad. It serves its purpose
in our developmental process causing us to set stretch goals,
develop our talents, and push the limits of our personal
capabilities. It makes the wheels of commerce turn. It allows
us to build community, heal lives, educate, feed the hungry,
and innovate.

But when we come to the wall we must confront the
shadow side of our egos—the unloved parts of ourselves
such as greed or insecurity. We must face ourselves and
answer tough questions such as, "What have I been lying to
myself about?" and "What am I most afraid of?"

No matter how we come to the wall, the experience of it is the same. It stops us in our tracks and brings us to our knees, yet simultaneously holds the possibility for joy, release, and self-acceptance. At the wall we are forced to confront ourselves. If we choose to grow beyond it, we must begin the difficult, exhilarating, confusing, life-altering process of living in the question. We must trade in the safety of thinking we know and embrace the uncertainty of *not knowing* for a while, as is the case for my colleague whose story follows.

DR. RICHARD FRIEND'S STORY:
"Living In The Question"

I originally started out doing anti-oppression work. Justice and change were my passion. Entering corporate America, I discovered that you can't talk about "the oppressed," "justice," etc. I strayed from this focus in order to do OD [Organizational Development] work instead of a justice perspective because OD is broader, more inclusive as a framework for my work. Over the years, organizational success and making money, have captured my imagination. Now I find myself struggling with the concept of selling out. I am sitting with questions like: What values have I given up? What compromises have I made to sit at the corporate table? How much of me have I lost?

I am struggling internally with two sets of concerns— profits to pay my huge mortgage and support my lifestyle versus commitment to a cause. I depend on my work as a livelihood so I have to make certain choices about what agenda to push, when, and how. So I sometimes go along with corporations that are saying in effect "come in as a change agent, but don't change anything."

I am talented at what I do, and I do it well. Often when I'm doing my work I'm in the zone—the right words come, things are integrated and seamless and I'm prepared physically, psychologically, and emotionally for my work. But there is something else that's missing. I don't yet know what is the IT that would rekindle my passion.

It's like I've been walking along a Great Wall for years enjoying the scenery and living with the Big Question. I know there is something else on the other side, but I don't know what it is. My fear causes me to not push through to find out what's on the other side. Deciding to risk knowing is painful, but I suspect that once I make the decision it will be a great journey.

In the meantime, I'm reading a lot, talking to people, getting clarity, and getting ready. What's next? I just don't know. I might open an institute and create a space of learning for people who do oppression work to teach each other. I'll work in community with others in a way that is true to my spirit—creating a better world in a collaborative teaching space. To paraphrase Toni Morrison, I've got a book I want to read and it's not yet written, so I've got to write it.

As Richard's story demonstrates, work-related quandaries often surface as nagging questions that won't go away until we address them. We must remember that finding meaning can be messy. Getting to answers is a process that may take many years. There are few pat answers to the questions Richard poses. Each presents a dilemma—a new problem to be wrestled with, no matter which path he chooses. Richard cares deeply about eliminating oppression in all of its forms. He also enjoys the freedom to earn a good living and live an upscale lifestyle. These are not just problems to be solved. These are *polarities* to be *managed*, and the tension between these polarities can be painful.

In life, pain is a given. That doesn't mean we have to suffer. In our relationship with work it is important not to get so stuck in the pain that we miss the deeper meaning and the endless opportunities for personal and organizational renewal. Sometimes it is more important to know what questions we're living with than it is to know the answers right off the bat. In the meantime, we must be mindful of what the questions we encounter at the wall are trying to teach us.

The key lies in learning to forgive ourselves for being less than perfect and to embrace our shadow as a learning tool. Then we will be able to forgive others—our parents for the mistakes they made, our organizations for being less than perfect as well, and so forth. This opens the door to the next stage of personal power.

STAGE 5. POWER BY PURPOSE

This stage capitalizes on our diminished ego and interior freedom. At Stage Five we can accept our personal and professional calling in whatever way it appears. We are aware of our weaknesses and can admit them without shame. We are more comfortable with who we are and more confident of our choices. Success for us is just another way to serve others (but without burnout). We may see ourselves as servant leaders, behind the scenes but still influential. We are broad in our thinking, intuitive in our judgments, and humble enough to learn from a child, as this woman, "Bruce" Nolan's, story illustrates:

BRUCE NOLAN'S STORY
"From The Mouths of Babes"

I was driving along one day several years ago with my five-year-old daughter. Suddenly from the back seat she blurted out, "You know, Mom, I figured out why people like me." She had been babbling on about this and that, and I had been half-listening the way parents sometimes do when they're driving or have other things on their minds. But that declaration stopped me in tracks. She got my attention. "Why do people like you, honey?" I was bursting with curiosity about what a five-year-old might have to say about such a serious subject. She said, "Because I like myself."

That was a pivotal moment for me. It got me thinking about myself, my work, and how people view themselves at work. I think workplaces take away that sense of self that my five-year-old had. They stomp it out of us with performance reviews that focus on what's wrong, that fail to acknowledge people's gifts and talents. So many people lose their self-esteem at work.

I made a conscious decision to not let that happen to me. I decided to devote my work life to empowering others as well. That is my purpose. A lot of people where I work today think I'm an executive. My behavior confuses

> them. I'm not an executive. I disregard the hierarchy. I'm
> not disrespectful; I just choose to break away from organi-
> zational myths in order to offer the best I have to offer. I
> discovered that org charts don't matter. There are very few
> consequences from breaking away. I am here to serve, and
> I am passionate about what I feel called to do. If I have an
> idea I share it. Who I am is not where I am on the organi-
> zational chart. I cannot give my best if I am confined to a
> box on the org chart. We are more than a "reporting
> relationship."

Bruce has begun to live Stage Five values in her work. Whether this stage is her home base developmentally or not, she stands in her power when she models these values. She is a leader, not in the sense implied by organizational charts, but a servant leader who, through introspection, takes the difficult journey to her own core and is willing to help others do the same.

At Stage Five we embrace purpose; are clearer about our personal vision, values, and direction; less self-serving and able to see and serve our organizations or our community more clearly. To move to Stage Six, Hagberg teaches, we need to have more faith and put much more on the line. In her words, this involves "peace amidst suffering, commitment to the journey, obedience to one's spiritual calling, and sacrifice."

STAGE 6. POWER BY WISDOM

Sixes are the sages of the universe. At Stage Six the clarity of purpose and commitment begun in Stage Five deepens. Now we are connected to our spiritual Source at all times and become wisdom figures and informal teachers of others.

At Stage Six we fear nothing, so we can act on principles that require deep courage. Our path is peaceful, even through pain. We are only concerned that we fulfill our calling in all places in our lives, as integrated and authentic people.

Sixes are quiet in service and transcendent. This does not mean that Stage Sixes are cloistered away. Quite the contrary. Sixes are active in the world. However at stage six we relate to people from a stance of compassion and service. Stage Six is marked by an absence of striving, a lack of interest in power, and a willingness to let go and trust the process of life unfolding.

Whether participating in a huge movement to right social injustice, or attempting to change the way business is done globally, or simply rearing our grandchildren, Sixes do what they do passionately and with deep caring and commitment.

This six-stage model of personal power offers a useful lens for looking at how we relate to work. It shows us how, by journeying inward, we perform from a stance of real power in which we bring our values, our true voice, our purpose, and our passion to work. This last invitation asks you to explore what it will take to move boldly in this direction.

INVITATION
Let Go to Discover
Real Power at Work

In *Real Power: Stages of Personal Power In Organizations*, Janet Hagberg describes Stages One through Three as "building up" and Stages Four through Six as "letting go." It is as if in the first three stages we are filling up our vessels as we build self-esteem, learn the ropes, and hone our personal skills. Then, as we continue to grow in our power, we experience a shift away from those outer concerns.

We are pulled to journey inward; and to do so we must empty our vessels. In the emptying, we let go of our ego's need to be strong, competent, or seemingly perfect. We create a sacred void where we can come to rediscover and embrace our true selves—imperfections and all.

As we make the transition from external to internal power we must anticipate—indeed create—an inner crisis where we face our fears and relinquish our egos. We must forgive ourselves and others as well. Only then can we begin to discover real power and the glimpses of wisdom it brings. It helps to seek wise counsel from those who have modeled the way and to plan time to be alone and reflect on ourselves.

In your journal explore the following questions:

1. What do you have to release in order to make room for your inner power to begin to emerge at work?

2. What external obstacles might get in the way?

3. What risk are you willing to take to stand more fully in your power?

4. Where and to whom might you turn for support?

PART IV

The Peace Pact:
Terms of Engagement

TEN

Make Peace with Your Fears

No one is exempt from the feelings of powerlessness that feed our fear at work. World-renowned scientists in academia fear losing their funding in a climate of tight budgetary constraints. Managers fear looking inept in the face of bad decisions. Corporate leaders fear their day-to-day choices might send company stocks plummeting. Decision-makers withhold sensitive information for fear the rank and file can't handle knowing.

Some supervisors pretend to know exactly what they're doing when they haven't a clue. They fear losing their credibility and, therefore, their clout. Imagine how refreshing it would be if mangers would occasionally admit "we're making this up as we go. This is uncharted territory for which we have no history, therefore, no roadmaps. We're counting on you for your best ideas!" But this rarely happens because most of us who are called to lead feel compelled to mask our fears and vulnerabilities with bravado.

Each merger, each downsizing, every organizational restructuring brings workers at every level face to face with their vulnerability, throwing us back to Stage One: Powerlessness. This is because such changes trigger our deepest fear—the fear of separation. In a 2004 Gallup Poll, 61 percent of Americans said they fear job loss due to outsourcing. Whether we happen to be part of the senior management team in charge, or an hourly worker waiting for marching orders, the prospect of being ousted throws us back to Stage One where we confront our feelings of Powerlessness and our dependence on the organization.

At such times we tend to avoid risk-taking. We become guarded as we brace ourselves for the worst. We may slip into a compliance mode, eager to please, cautious not to rock the boat until the storm passes and we can regain our equilibrium. We fear being snatched out of our comfort zones. We fear not knowing, looking foolish, or being found out as imposters pretending to know.

At its worst, our fear creates havoc, blocking our creativity, stifling productivity, and leaving us to behave in ways that are disempowering or inept. We may refrain from saying what we really think in a staff meeting for fear our opinions might ruffle the feathers of the powers that be, rendering us jobless. Instead we hold "parking lot meetings" after the meeting, sharing our observations and offering up critiques in the presence of our peers. In this safer setting we can speak our truths—the positions that we fear might cost us our jobs if muttered in the presence of managers who hold our fate in their hands. We fear losing our jobs.

At times we even fear our fears. And in our fearfulness we reach out for someone to blame. For as long as we can point the finger elsewhere we do not have to face the added fear of facing ourselves and our own culpability. Fear and blame become twin brothers at work. They work against us destroying trust, stifling creativity, and impeding healthy high performing work relationships. An inappropriate response when fears present themselves blocks from our view the choices and possibilities before us.

To make peace with our work, we must first make peace with our fears. We must be willing to risk failing, to ask for help, and to discover new skills or attitudes that we can shore up in order to survive and thrive.

Julia Cameron, in her beautiful book *Walking in This World*, invites us to see fear as a friend—as a welcome visitor who nudges us to examine ourselves and to take a closer look at our situation. Fear is not a ghoulish monster waiting to devour us. What devours us is our *response* to the fears that crop up in the course of our day-to-day living.

Recent research in the medical scientific community has confirmed what our spiritual teachers have always known: mind and body work as one. As we think, so we are. What we believe, we become. If we are governed by fearful thoughts, we become timid, powerless workers who refuse to take the risks needed for growth, creativity, and personal fulfillment. If we fear that our ideas won't matter, we never reveal them. So we learn nothing about our true capabilities and the organization suffers because it never has access to the best we have to offer. If we think people can't be trusted, then we approach our work relationships fearful that people are out to get us. The choices we then make—becoming defensive, avoiding friendships, hoarding information instead of sharing—all guarantee that what we believe becomes true.

As discussed throughout this book, we are confronted by a crisis of meaning at predictable points in our lives. It may come when our soul beckons us to answer a call to more authenticity in our lives or because we can no longer hide from ourselves. At times the crisis is associated with a catastrophic life event such as an illness or layoff, which forces us to stop and reckon with our work and our lives. But just as often it is prodded by an inner upheaval that comes quietly out of the blue, unattached to any particular life event that we can pinpoint. Novelist Zora Neal Hurston in *Their Eyes Were Watching God* captured this inner crisis eloquently, "Something fell off the shelf inside of me and I had to go inside to rearrange things."

To rearrange things on our inner shelves, we must face our fears. A thirty-six-year-old client of mine experienced what some might describe as a meteoric rise to the top of his game. Suddenly he looked around and the only position he could vie for in his current organization is that of his boss, the chief executive. Alarmed that he had plateaued so quickly, he began to explore his options elsewhere. He is very marketable, but earns a salary that is well above what the market outside of his current company will bear. What to do? The idea of simply coasting—enjoying the ride to see where it goes is rather alarming to this young man. He fears that if he lingers too long in his present job, somehow he will miss the boat. In his thinking, success means knowing his next moves and never becoming stagnant. He wants to continue climbing higher and higher, getting positions with increasing decision-making responsibility. If his organization doesn't come up with a clever plan to capture his imagination, he is ready to move on. His resume is ready. He is keeping his networks alive in preparation for a possible move out of his organization at any time.

What I find most profound as I talk with this individual is that he truly loves his current job and can think of very little else he'd rather be doing right now. Yet his fears about possibly having "topped out" prompt him to move on— away from where he is happiest.

At thirty-six his fears are fueled by personal goals like paying off enormous student loans, raising his family of five, and laying the groundwork to be financially solvent later in life. In talking with him, I discovered that he does not feel he has the luxury to simply coast—to simply enjoy what he is presently doing and to trust that things will work out. As we talked, he paced back and forth wrestling with a flood of different emotions, some contradictory as he tries to figure out how best to excel, how to gauge whether and when to move on. Finally I asked what would it take to for him to simply be where he is. His answer came quickly, "assurances that my company cares enough about me to *guarantee* me a future, and I know where all the bodies are buried. I know they can't promise me that." Then he goes on to offer an important lesson in reality, "I am, after all, the boss of my work life."

While this young professional may seem restless, he is aware of who is ultimately in charge of his life—himself. As he continues to mature, this attitude will serve him well.

His antennae are up waiting to get clues about what tactical moves he needs to make. He reacts to his fears with appropriate questions: Does this work still work for me given my goals, needs, and direction? Can I continue to leverage my strengths here? And while my own idealism might lead me to advise him to coast, basking in the treasures of his present work experience, he is not in crisis—not held hostage by fear.

The crisis comes when we sense that things no longer make sense the way they are, and we are paralyzed by fear, unable to move or to take steps to transform our work experience in some way. Perhaps we desire more depth in our work or more security. Perhaps we are "rusting out"—feeling under challenged or underutilized. Or we may have experienced a loss such as being passed over for a promotion we deserved.

Our response to fear has been labeled the "stress response." It affects us physically, evoking 1,400 different bodily changes ranging from elevated heartbeat and the release of cortisol into the blood stream initially, to hardening of the arteries and heart attacks long term. The stress response begins with our thinking: "I'm not enough." "They will annihilate my career if I speak my truth."

> "There are people who shape their lives by the fear of death and others who shape their lives by the joy of life."
>
> —CHARLES HANDY

"I'm too old to change jobs." It quickly shapes our moods; dictates our behaviors; dampens our sex drive, our creativity, and our hopes; and alters our life choices and the quality of life of those around us.

Fear is an instinct—a built-in survival mechanism that warns us of danger. It can be experienced in dysfunctional ways, or it can be a useful early warning system.

If you are walking around at work feeling fearful, it could be that something *is*, in fact, amiss. Our fear is sometimes an invitation to pull the blinders off our eyes and discover the source of a perceived threat. Our fear could be a warning that we are trapped in the wrong job. It could be linked to the anxiety one feels when one's voice is being silenced. Once you identify the root causes of your fear, you can take steps to make things right. Managing fear teaches us how to be courageous in the face of difficulties.

Once we face and befriend our fears, we can go beyond them, striking out into a path that is true to who we are. This is how David Whyte describes the initial steps of the journey of embracing fear and using it as a catalyst to move toward greater wholeness and personal power.

Following our path is, in effect, a kind of going off the path, through open country. There is a certain early stage when we are left to camp out in the wilderness, alone, with few supporting voices. Out there in the silence we must build a hearth, gather the twigs, and strike the flint for the fire ourselves.

Choosing to walk through our fears and into the unknown is scary business. It leaves us vulnerable to those who look askance at nonconformity. It poses the possibility of loss, and it exposes us to those who might exploit us. But it is a necessary step if we are to make peace with our work. By naming our fears, confronting, and making friends with them, we can take the necessary steps to harness our power and make choices that are congruent with what our souls need at work. Here is the story of one man's journey to the other side of his fears.

BOB CHOBIN'S STORY:
"The Road Less Traveled"

I've always had a fear of not reaching my goal, not finishing what I start or of failing. All my life I have been driven, always preparing, always wanting to be the best. This was especially true during the early years of building my career.

I worked my way up to the position of lead IT specialist with about fifteen direct reports. As I matured and started thinking about retirement, I began to see things differently. Who has the real power in my company? It's not the managers, but the workers on the front line. My company, IBM, was getting the best information from the people on the front line. I got called upon as a specialist and came to realize my power. I realized that without us workers the company would grind to a halt.

I also realized that companies can pull our strings like puppeteers. As I became more self-aware, I began taking more risks. I started cutting the strings. I had had a series of successes. The company recognized my worth. I started questioning things more openly and with much success.

My company is very open to telecommuting, so I now telecommute from home. I'm on conference calls daily with my direct reports and others. IBM benefits by achieving more diversification. They can pull together a matrix of experts from all over and get the right people together tapping world-wide talents. I work less intensely but much smarter than before. I go for the big things that matter, not just the piddly things that go nowhere. It's harder to get recognized when you work from home. But that's less important to me now.

What's important is to step out of the box and trust your inner wisdom and your expertise. Some managers manage by fear. They are controlling and power-driven. I am no longer ruled by such behaviors.

I learned that one has to risk failing in order to free oneself of the company strings. My advice to young professionals is that companies are always weeding through people looking for talent. Your job is to be prepared to offer your best. You must study hard, build your skills, and do your best work. Then take the risk to try things differently. It's a gamble, but it's well worth it. Don't live in fear of losing your job. Such fear disempowers you and causes you to get stuck. In this climate of downsizing it's easy to get fearful and to feel that you're not worth that much. The thing we shouldn't forget is the company needs us. Look within yourself and say, "I'm not insignificant. I'm good, and I have something to offer a company that appreciates me."

In hindsight, I wish I had the wisdom in my thirties to shore up myself financially so I could have taken the risks to free myself earlier in life.

Going off the beaten path on to the road less traveled has put Bob in touch with a whole new way of seeing and doing work. While not all organizations offer the flexibility Bob has found at IBM, most are beginning to experiment with new ways of designing work and work relationships. Many, like me, feel that the new models of workplaces for the twenty-first century will, of necessity, be more inclusive, more worker-friendly, and more flexible because employees will demand this as a condition for remaining. As we rethink our relationship with work, it will help to face our traditional work-related fears, as Bob has done, and to explore alternatives that allow us to do and be our best as workers.

COMMITMENT ONE:
TAME YOUR FEARS

Most us of have deep wells of potential that are never tapped because fears—some valid, most imagined—become obstacles to our greatness.

Real fears are useful. They protect us from bad choices and may even save our lives. Without doubt there are times when our intuition and logic rightly caution us, "Don't do this; it's threatening to your safety and well-being."

Most fears, however, are just plain worry about some imagined possibility that may never materialize. Such fears are neither useful, nor healthy. I polled several people, asking the simple question, "What do you fear the most at work." Some had genuine concerns about being squeezed out in an impending merger. The majority, though, were preoccupied with everyday human missteps. They feared making a mistake, missing an important deadline, or drawing a blank at the speaker's podium. Some were masters at escalating, "I will botch my presentation of the quarterly engineering update to senior management, look foolish and incompetent to my peers and superiors, be fired, and blacklisted in my field, never to work again." Harboring such worries, and the fantasies around them, serve no useful purpose. They simply block creativity and spontaneity and diminish the joy of our work experience.

ACTION IDEAS:

1. Make a list of the fears that crop up at work for you.

2. Next to each fear, indicate whether it is (V) valid or (I) imagined.

3. Pick one fear that is valid. Plan a strategy and action steps for minimizing the likelihood of this fear materializing.

4. Pick one fear that is imagined. Challenge yourself in the following ways:

- Test your assumptions in the real world. Pick a challenge where the stakes are relatively low. Feel the fear and do it anyway. See what happens.

- Counter your imagined fear with logic by pushing it to the limit ("I might get fired and never be hired again," or "I might die of embarrassment"). Then you can easily dismiss it, for you know that won't happen.

- Practice countering a debilitating worrisome fear with an opposite positive affirmation. For example, if you think, "I might draw a blank when I get up to give my presentation," counter that thought with, "They asked me to present because I have the information and expertise they want." This will shift your attention from yourself and your fear to the audience and its needs that you can fill.

ELEVEN

Get Support

When you picked up this book, perhaps you were searching for a means to heal some aspect of your work. You made a choice, consciously or not, to find support for your efforts. I have had the repeated experience of deciding to make a change in some area of my life, only to have a friend hand me just the right piece of information, or refer me to a book or to someone who gives me just the support I need. The people around us, are co-creators of our work and life experiences. Books, as instruments of people's ideas, are a part of the mix as well. The mind of the writer joins with the minds of everyone she has ever known or touched or read or listened to. Shaped by these relationships and life experiences, the writer chooses, or is chosen, to offer up her insights in print so others can share in that knowing. The book itself becomes not just the writer's work, but also the work of the collective.

In this spirit, I have shared many stories of real people and their challenges and triumphs in making peace with their work. Long after you have completed reading this book, my hope is you will be more tuned in to the rich resources that Joseph Campbell referred to as "a thousand unseen hands," that appear to help us daily with our lifetime endeavors. Many have successfully created what we seek. Their stories are filled with inspiration and useful information if we take the time to notice and to invite them into our lives.

I start with books as one place people turn for support. The reason people sometimes reach first for a book when they are trying to transform themselves is that this is a private, impersonal way of accessing ideas and help. People, especially high achievers, are often reluctant to reach out for help. Pride, upbringing, humiliation, a high need for control, or just plain embarrassment about asking for help are among the reasons people don't ask for support.

The *Wall Street Journal* ran a story June 22, 2004, about CEOs beginning to seek support from psychotherapists as they face increasing pressures in their jobs. Journalist Carol Hymowitz had this to say about their choice, "The stigma about mental illness persists, so most keep their sessions secret. But unlike earlier generations of executives, today's CEOs know they don't have to be falling apart to seek help." She then quotes Psychoanalyst Robert Michels who assures readers, "CEOs have the same relationship problems and life-stage issues as the rest of us." This is an interesting perspective, especially when you consider that, for all of us,

a crisis of meaning in our work is one of the most predictable life-stage dilemmas. Few can afford the time and money
required to get support of this caliber. But arguably, support
is a key ingredient in any change and particularly in changing our work life experience. I got support from Donna
Bennett, who is a practicing therapist and coach, as I rear-
ranged the pieces of my own work. We worked through a
ten-month process called "The Leadership Journey."
Recently, I put this question to Donna as a helping professional, "Where does the helper turn for help?"

DONNA BENNETT'S STORY:
"Turning to One Another for Support"

In my experience as a psychotherapist and career coach,
people typically don't seek the support they need. Women
are more likely than men to eventually ask for help. They
feel an obligation to do it all, and they are concerned about
work/life balance. Men, when they do seek support, tend
to look at particulars: "My relationship isn't working."
"I'm losing my job." "I want to change jobs." I take them
into their broader life and help them to see how all the
parts are connected.

When things get really hectic, I turn to a coach who is
also a therapist. But I don't stop there. I also rely on some
key friends who will listen without judging. There are
times when I turn to people with particular expertise: orga-
nizers, colleagues in my networks, and so forth. There are
four or five people that I turn to for different things. One
is my prayer partner. One is an individual who always com-

pliments me. One is a woman who is very wise and very serious with whom I discuss deep subjects. One is a friend with whom I'm writing and illustrating a book together. She is my creative "board member." Then there are professionals like my life coach, my friend who is my spiritual guide and co-instructor in the Leadership Journey course at the university. My youngest son is a wonderful writer and computer tech person. He supports me by critiquing and editing my work. My husband, daughters, sons, and my granddaughter are also part of my support network, regularly offering their perspective and creative input. They believe in me. I also regularly set up coffee or lunches in my professional network so I don't feel isolated.

Knowing who you are, knowing what you value and looking at your work and all aspects of your life: spiritual, community, significant others, friends, families, and so forth are important. If we align our values with the significant areas of our lives, it will spill over into other relationships. If you hate your job, what about it do you hate? Let's say your boss always asks you to work late and work overtime, but never gives you time for training. Your values are personal growth. Ask, "What is my role in creating this situation? What choices do I have? What steps have I taken to make things better. Is it time to transfer out or quit? What's realistic given my life obligations?" And most important, "What support do I need?"

When there is a crisis, I get help from my inner Spiritual source and from reaching out for help. When I was director of counseling at Colonial Church, our numbers went down after 9/11, so we didn't meet our budget. We were short money. We went to the board and asked for donations. They said no. They talked to lay leaders of the church. One, a businessman, said the church can't help. After many meetings the church decided to shut down the center. That was a personal blow.

Guided by prayer and faith, I put a plan together to show them how they could keep the center going and a proposal to make that happen. They didn't like it. So I put together a proposal for how to close things down over time. I continued to counsel people; I brought in a community speaker, set a budget, generated funds, paid the church, and proposed severance pay for myself. I then put together my own practice by turning to my networks—sending notices out to everyone I know. That was over six years ago, and things are going well. I did it all by networking, by word of mouth, by staying positive, working hard, and taking risks. It continues to pay off. I just got a new job teaching at the University of Minnesota, and I'm sixty-eight years old with a master's degree.

Getting support works best when we make it a conscious choice to attract or create the presence of others who support us in our work. Years ago I attended a stress management retreat in the beautiful mountain town of Berkley Springs, West Virginia. The Spa was great, my participants were good people to be with, and so was our facilitator, John D. Adams. But the only thing I remembered fifteen years later was the idea he planted that each of us should convene a personal board of directors. A personal board of directors is a group of people you call on to provide feedback, guidance, and support for your efforts. In the years that I have used the idea, I have added those who are credible at modeling the way by living the values I am drawn to. Today my personal board of directors includes a spiritual coach; a financial planner; a masseuse/holistic healer; a son and daughter-in-law who, as young adults, bring wonderful perspective to my life and my decisions; five close colleagues in my field; a bookkeeper who adores the details, which I hate; and a few "best friends" who tell me the truth and cheer me on, even when others think I'm pursuing a hare-brained scheme.

I can hear you saying, "I've got many such helpful relatives, friends, and colleagues in my life." This is true. Life provides us with natural support—anyone such as family, friends, coworkers, and sometimes even strangers who help us. However, a personal board of directors is a group you enlist, in a conscious, deliberate way because they embody skills and perspectives we might lack. Many of the people in my personal board of directors are there because they excel at skills I lack. Their help frees me up to play to my strengths, rather than struggle with something for which I have little aptitude.

To maximize the impact of your personal board of directors you must (1) Choose people who embody virtues, skills, or perspectives you lack, or who can provide assistance with things you have no time or ability to do well. (2) Get their agreement to play this role in your life and their commitment to tell you the truth. They must be active, willing participants—honored and happy to do so. (3) Be conscious of these helpers as your first line of support, so that in a pinch you quickly and effortlessly know where to turn to get the feedback, ideas, or support you need. (4) Be willing to reciprocate in the relationship, either through pay for those serving as professionals or by extending your-self on their behalf as well.

I have found that being conscious and intentional about enlisting these key players in shaping my work life brings exponential results compared to going it alone or relying on the wrong people.

COMMITMENT TWO:
REACH OUT FOR HELP

Getting support takes many forms. Unfortunately it is, for many, a difficult habit to cultivate. The suggestions that follow are just a few ways to begin to let go, reach beyond the ego's need to go it alone, and position ourselves to work smarter and get better results both personally and professionally.

ACTION IDEAS:

1. Identify a change you're trying to make in your work right now. Who are role models— people you know personally who have successfully completed a similar change? Who are possible cheerleaders who believe in you and delight in offering words of encouragement? Who can offer expert technical assistance? Who are likely mentors, wise ones, or spiritual guides who will provide feedback, counsel, and listen non-judgmentally? While you're pursing your work-related change, consider your physical well-being also. A fitness trainer might have a role to play in helping you get the stamina needed to face what's ahead. Or you may need to shore up other aspects of your well-being with the help of a physician, financial advisor, or a once-monthly housekeeper.

2. Using your answers to these questions put together a personal "Board of Directors"

comprised of people who are in your corner and can support you in your efforts. Know what you can afford to pay for and where you may need to ask for kindness or barter for services. Approach each one and ask for help. Be specific in what you ask of them. Then see what happens.

3. Join a support network of like-minded people seeking to transform their work.

4. Find a mentor, either formally or informally, and enlist their guidance in some aspect of your work or life.

5. Learn to barter services. Over the years, I have had access to services I couldn't otherwise afford, and built friendships in the process, by simply bartering my expertise in exchange for another person's.

TWELVE

Strengthen Your Positive Core

One of the most exciting aspects of work life is the drive to excel. This is why Stage Three: Power by Achievement on the Hagberg model is such a satisfying and important stage in our growth towards real power. This drive is an inborn survival skill. A baby struggles to pick up an object and place it in its mouth. Patiently, painstakingly day after day the baby practices. Mistakes become feedback. The practice becomes disciplined, and, eventually, the baby gets it right, bouncing up and down with squeals of joy. The infant continues the practice again and again—hand to object, to mouth until he or she perfects the skill. Intuitively the baby knows the formula: stick with what works and do it better and better. This is the key to achievement, and with it comes the joy of work—deep satisfaction based on competence, self-discovery, and eventually service to others.

True success is figuring out what works for you—physically, emotionally, and spiritually—

and making daily choices to do more of what works for you. It also involves knowing when things no longer work and being willing to reassess and reinvent our work lives continually. Diana Whitney, a pioneer in the field of Appreciative Inquiry speaks of the importance of discovering and working from our "positive core." By definition, Appreciative Inquiry is *a cooperative search for the best that people and their organizations have to offer.* Here is her personal story of using this approach to redefine personal success and make peace with her work as a leading scholar and international consultant.

DIANA WHITNEY'S STORY:
"Working with My Positive Core"

Making peace with my work is also about making peace with myself—discovering what's really going on with me right now. What are my strengths and what are my unfulfilled dreams? I have begun to realize that one aspect of my work that I used to love is no longer as life-giving as it used to be. I'm competent at it and could continue to do it well, but it just doesn't nurture me right now. As I become honest with what I know about myself and what my dreams are, I must rethink whether, or how, I want to do this aspect of my work.

Using the appreciative approach, I start with my positive core—my strengths, capabilities, hopes, and dreams. Doing inquiry brings this positive core to light. Our positive core isn't static. A job that is wonderful at one point in our life may not be so wonderful at another time. My work is different today from a year ago. What worked last year might not work today. I must discover who I am NOW.

First, I focus on discovery. I ask questions about what gives me joy. What work have I done that I love. I do a root cause analysis of relationships, tasks, and authority. What motivates me?

Then I dream. The dreaming phase has to be bigger than oneself, bigger than life. I dream about the world and what my calling is, what can I contribute. That stimulates me.

Then I move to the design phase. This recognizes that I have lots of choices, and I have to make choices. How much traveling do I want to do? What industry do I want to work with? What kinds of relationships do I want to create? It's important to get my intention articulated, so that in the process I can embody this intention.

Finally, the destiny phase. Here my work involves trusting that if I ask the right questions of myself and other people about what's good for me, it's going to manifest. That's a law of the universe. To quote a pastor who has given me guidance, "We must pray as if it's all up to God and live as if it's all up to us."

Making peace with our work is always a relational process—it must always be done in dialogue with others. As the saying goes, "we are made and imagined in the eyes of one another." Just as we're having this dialogue right now with one another, it's helping us both clarify our identity and strengthen our personal and professional relationship. We are both living in the same time and learning together how to be successful at work and life.

The field of Appreciative Inquiry (AI) has taught me the most about how to recast work and our workplace endeavors in the light of its positive core, so we learn from what works and we see what's possible. I use this approach in strategic planning sessions, in diversity work, in team-building sessions, in leadership development efforts, in program evaluations, and wherever else I can with clients because the Appreciative approach supports healthy, collaborative work environments. Rather than viewing organizations as problems to be solved, AI views organizations as sources of unlimited potential. Rather than posing questions of pain ("What are we doing wrong, and who is to blame?"), it poses questions of possibilities ("What are we best at, and how can we carry forward the best we have to offer?").

As Diana's story reminds us, what we focus on, what we dream of becomes our reality. It is also important to discover and carry forward the *best parts* of what has worked for us in the past.

Imagine the possibilities if we apply the philosophy of Appreciative Inquiry to all aspects of our work lives. What are you already successful at—what do you already do *right* in your work, in your life? What reality are you zeroing in on as you deepen and heal your work life? What questions of possibilities might you pose as you make peace with your work? Thinking and acting from this stance allows us to move beyond the daily grind to experience the gratitude in our customers' eyes when we solve a problem or beat a deadline. We can notice what management and employees do *right*. Instead of simply heaving a sigh of relief on completing a tough project for a client, we can allow ourselves to fully experience the satisfaction of a job well done.

Looking at work from this angle, we can see work challenges as spiritually enriching. We can face the demanding rough spots with the questions, "How does this make me stronger?" "Where are the opportunities for growing or making wiser choices?" From an Appreciative viewpoint we come to experience work as privileged service and, at the same time, know that we are never stuck—especially when the only way forward is out. At such times the act of moving on can be a positive choice where we take the best we have to offer into our new beginnings.

My friend Stephen, a real estate broker, guffaws with embarrassment each time we point out to him how masterful he is at building friendships and putting people together. Yet, in spite of his success in sales and in business and the lasting relationships he has forged with people from all walks of life, he truly doesn't see himself that way. On a vacation with family and friends, our cruise liner docked for a few hours at a tiny, remote Mexican fishing village. Within minutes, Stephen had made friends with the owner and servers in a small dive that served the best fried fish I've ever tasted. Stephen, who speaks no Spanish at all, was invited back into the kitchen where he was having a lively conversation with dozens of his new *amigos* (the only Spanish word he knows), some of whom spoke no English at all. Like the Pied Piper touting his magical flute, he led scores of family members, friends, and other tourists into the little restaurant, and the crowds swelled spilling out onto the beach behind the restaurant as we devoured platefuls of the fish. Making friends and facilitating connections is Stephen's greatest strength, yet he is often unaware of the presence and the power of this talent. He dismisses our feedback by saying, "Doesn't everybody do that?" No, we assure him, everybody doesn't do that.

Lately, I've been coaching Stephen to see his impact on others as a talent, and to be intentional about nurturing this gift and using it in a most positive way to continue to serve others as he builds a thriving business and coaches his staff to be their best. Here are some guidelines that I have found helpful for myself and others.

I. MAKE NOTE OF WHAT PEOPLE REGULARLY COMPLIMENT YOU ON.

Instead of dismissing the feedback we get from others about our strengths, look for evidence of these behaviors in different situations and relationships. This is important since most of the time our strengths come to the fore in relationship with others. What attributes and skills did your parents, teachers, and others regularly compliment you on?

My client Elaine always excelled in sports. By the time she entered college, she had amassed numerous medals and awards for a range of sports activities. She loved the discipline of practice, the adrenalin rush of competition, and she loved winning. Over time, she also learned how to lose gracefully. Today she brings these strengths to her role as CEO of a health care organization. In a recent interview of high achievers, when asked to identify the secret to her success, she immediately answered, "My athletic abilities and training."

2. LOOK FOR HIDDEN STRENGTHS THAT LIE BEHIND YOUR WEAKNESSES.

This shouldn't be hard to do since we are generally quicker to name our weaknesses than to celebrate our strengths. Sometimes when I coach people to own their strengths, I invite them to pick a weakness, flip it over, and see whether a strength lies on the other side. Let's say your weakness is you tend to be impatient with people who move slowly at work. Could it be that you are a task-oriented go-getter who can always be counted on to get things done on time under pressure? To grow, you would need to balance your strength of efficiency with self-management and patience in dealing with people whose strengths and weaknesses are different from yours.

Jonathan, a former coworker of mine, always finished last. He was often the brunt of jokes at work for he walked slowly, spoke slowly, and was always measured and analytical in his responses. Jonathan was aware of his "weakness," often apologizing for taking so long. Sarcastically, people referred to him as "Speedy" behind his back. Once at lunch someone made a comment about Jonathan's "analysis paralysis." His supervisor overheard and, smart woman that she is, quickly came to Jonathan's defense, explaining, "There are certain projects around here that he is most well-suited for because he leaves no stone unturned. He is thorough, earnest, and accurate. I can count on him to get it right every time."

Consider another example of strengths hidden behind a weakness, revealed in a recent dialogue with my client Brandy:

Brandy: I am a procrastinator. My procrastination gets me into all kinds of problems. The worst thing about it is that even though I tell myself that I do my best work under pressure, I'm always left feeling I could have done a better job if I'd started my project earlier.

Delorese: What might be a strength that lurks on the other side of your procrastination?

Brandy: Well, I want to do things right. So I get anxious, worrying that I won't be able to do my best. I tell myself I need to do more research or I clean my office first or I convince myself that I don't have the right skills to do it perfectly.

Delorese: So you want things to be perfect.

Brandy: Even as a kid, I had to get A's.

Delorese: Why was that?

Brandy: Well, I was real smart and my parents knew it and would accept nothing less.

Delorese: Did you procrastinate back in school?

Brandy: Yes, but I was still able to get A's because I'm a quick study. Later in college, I majored in and took courses in whatever came easily to me, so I continued to get A's even though I did put off studying until the night before a test.

As we talked further, the strengths hidden behind Brandy's procrastination revealed themselves. She is very smart—a quick study, and paradoxically, her tendency to procrastinate is fueled by a yearning for excellence. To flip the coin of procrastination to the other side, I gave Brandy two self-talk principles to practice: "Done is better than perfect," and "I will no longer confuse perfection with excellence." Over time she may come to replace the fear of failing that drives her procrastination with her love of excellence. As she does so, she will become increasingly likely to tackle tasks in a timely way.

3. Do more of what energizes you—what makes you feel most alive or causes you to lose track of time.

Sometimes our strengths show up as a feeling of aliveness associated with some activity we do so well; we could do it in our sleep and forever. Is there something that compels you? That fires you up? It could be a hobby, or some aspect of your job, or a role such as parenting or helping someone work through a personal problem that feeds your soul and fuels your passion. It could be your love of teamwork and the fact that you can't wait to join a group where you can apply your skills to do great creative things collectively.

4. Pay attention to what you repeatedly feel called to do.

Sometimes our unacknowledged strengths show up as a nagging question in our heads that never goes away. "When are you going to get back to your photography?" "How come you don't practice the piano anymore?" These callings stirring within us are impulses that can guide us to make more fulfilling choices in our work. More often than not they are linked to our strengths. For me the call to write surfaces regularly. I'm most alive at the keyboard. I get lost in the moment. My concerns about bills or life struggles and even time all slip away, giving way to pure joy. If I stop writing for long periods of time, a dullness settles into my days. The only thing that revives me is to return to my journal or my keyboard. Writing feeds my self-esteem and affirms my values, my motives, and my identity. It is part of my positive core. I rely heavily on it to sustain me and my work.

5. REMEMBER YOUR STRENGTHS ARE PORTABLE.

Once you unveil and own your strengths, you can enjoy the thrill and benefits of taking your strengths wherever you go. This will go a long way towards enriching your work experience. Here is how one CEO modeled the way by living her values and playing to her strengths.

Chris Harper, M.D., was the hospital's fifth CEO in eleven years. With each CEO that had come and gone, employees had to deal with a new senior administrative team, new strategic initiatives, and so forth. They were jaded by the lack of leadership continuity, and their morale, performance, and productivity were negatively impacted. The new CEO, anxious to break the cycle of aborted leadership, conducted a series of focus groups to gather feedback. She listened carefully to comments like, "We feel the CEO position here is a pass-through assignment," or "No one cares enough to stick with us long enough to succeed."

Dr. Harper then called an all-hands meeting at which she reflected back what she heard, announced her plans, and promised to stay for the long haul. Her first official act was to institute a "partners in change" process in which she engaged employees at every level, as well as former patients and suppliers, in shaping the hospital's transformation. After several months of skepticism, employees began to make note of the consistency with which the CEO followed through on her promise. They reported a noticeable difference in senior leadership's behaviors and commitment levels. They expressed appreciation for minor details such as the fact that when Dr. Harper walked the halls she would greet employees who had attended her focus groups by name. She would routinely ask employees, "How are you doing?" "Are there any problems I should be aware of?" As of this writing, four years later, the CEO continues to be one of the most admired executives the hospital has known. The hospital has survived a difficult merger with another institution led by this woman and her staff. Throughout the transition period she continued to earn the trust and support of employees system-wide.

When I interviewed Dr. Harper, I joked about a stereotypical comment someone had made about physicians being tough as leaders. "I see it differently," she said, "the most important strength I bring comes from years of listening carefully to patients in order to make the right diagnosis. That's the skill I rely on most in my role as an administrator."

I was reminded once again, that the strengths that form our positive core are transferable from situation to situation.

6. LEVERAGE WHAT YOU'RE BEST AT, MINIMIZE OR MANAGE YOUR WEAK POINTS.

If Madame Curie, Michael Jordan, or Bill Gates approached their work by identifying their weak points and trying to fix them, they would not be listed among the luminaries of high achievement today. Yet focusing on weaknesses is precisely how many of our supervisors go about trying to improve performance. They minimize our strengths, highlight our flaws, and tell us to go back to work and try harder.

According to Marcus Buckingham and Donald L. Clifton, authors of the bestseller, *Now, Discover Your Strengths,* companies spend more training time and dollars trying to eradicate employee deficits than they do on building existing strengths. Thanks to the work of such scholars and practitioners, "play to your strengths" has gone from being an age-old management cliché to being the best piece of advice these days for restoring a joyous, healthy relationship with our work.

In my work as a writer, when I focus on my weak points in crafting prose or the technicalities of spelling or on the limits of my thinking on a subject, I freeze. I become self-conscious and inept as writer's block sets in. To get going again, I have to remind myself to simply do what I do best. I thank God for spell check and remind myself there are editors whose strengths lie in scrutinizing and perfecting the final product. They will play to their strengths. I must play to mine.

"Worker's block" is a similar phenomenon. Some workers are so practiced in lamenting their weaknesses that they can't tell you what they are truly good at. (Thankfully, there are now self-assessment tools to help us find out.) They spend a lot of frustrating time trying to perfect something they will never be great at.

None of this is to suggest that we shouldn't seek new learning or eradicate debilitating habits. Quite the contrary: to hone a skill or tackle and transcend a difficult task can be energizing and confidence-building. But this is not the place to *start*. We each embody a particular combination of attributes—a unique set of abilities, values, motives, and behaviors that is ours and ours alone. Some people call it potential. I like to describe it as our greatness or our strengths. These strengths can help us navigate our lives and our work in ways that are satisfying and much easier than some of the traditional approaches to work. My music teacher used to coach the up-and-coming stars in our class to put themselves in situations where they are musically strongest and most comfortable. She believed they would more quickly and easily build their unique style from this comfort zone. She was right, and she gained national recognition for turning out an impressive number of top quality performers.

Our strengths give us the edge, make us create what we seek, allow us to serve others, and help build our sense of self-worth. Harnessing our strengths allows us to embrace our greatness and to more consistently connect with our full potential. This is important because to make peace with our work, we must be grounded on a solid platform of values and strengths that will steer our actions in the right direction for self and for our organization. Jim Collins, co-author of *Built to Last* and author of *Good to Great*, teaches us that successful companies achieve greatness by doing what they are best at in the world, what they are passionate about, and by making sure they do what drives their economic engine. These behaviors are important to the financial viability and the long-term sustainability of any venture. They can also serve us as individuals wanting to do and be our best as we make a living.

COMMITMENT THREE:
PLAY TO YOUR STRENGTHS

Think of the people in your life—your co-workers, family members, friends, managers, teachers you have had, your sports coach, your family physician. Each one, like you, has a particular set of attributes that makes him or her unique in the world. Each has a given disposition, character traits, and a way of seeing the world and of communicating with others, skill sets, acquired knowledge, and so forth.

Beyond that, we each have a talent or two we may even take for granted because it comes so easily to us. People may gravitate to you because you have a winning personality. While others agonize over a scheduling nightmare that requires coordinating the activities of a hundred people, you may have a real knack for whipping things together on an Excel spreadsheet in no time at all, much to the amazement of your colleagues. Such natural gifts combine with your skills to create the strengths you bring to the table as a worker. Leveraging what you do best—this positive core—is the key to building self-esteem and to deepening the joy in your work. But first, you must become consciously aware of these strengths, so you can bring them into play effectively. The ideas below will help.

ACTION IDEAS:

1. Schedule a meeting with your boss. Tell him or her you want a half-hour or so to get feedback about your strengths *only*, so you can begin to deepen these. (Make it clear that you do not want to talk about weakness in this meeting.)

2. To make action idea one more powerful and fun, offer to reciprocate. Suggest to your boss that you will do the same for him or her in return.

3. Schedule additional one-on-one or group meetings, especially with your staff or family members and ask them for a two-way strengths feedback session as well. (I tried this with a small group of colleagues recently and it turned into a heartfelt celebration of self and others that left us all buoyed up and ready to take on the world.)

4. Pursue continuing education. If your work place won't, or can't, support your training, find and fund your own workshops, seminars, or classes. Investing in yourself, especially in areas where your talents and inclinations lie, is a wonderful way to strengthen your core.

THIRTEEN

Write Your Own Success Story

Whose definition of success are you working off of? What is your vision for your work and your life? Are your choices moving you in the direction of your vision? How are you defining your work experience?

In the introduction to this book, I described the traditional formula for success: work hard, take on increasing amounts of responsibility, earn, spend, and save as much as possible, and make a difference locally or globally. In sharing my personal crisis and awakening, I described my confusion at scoring high on these success criteria externally, but not *feeling* successful internally. I now understand that our inner compass is the best gauge for what success truly is. Success in work may, at times, come at the expense of success in living. When that happens, are we truly successful?

Many of my clients tell me they relate to the story that follows.

JIM BROWN'S STORY:
"Facing the Shadow"

I was raised by a father whose work came first. He was a good man and really cared about his family in his own way. But, unfortunately, I saw very little of him growing up, and we didn't have a close relationship as a result. He believed that hard work was its own reward, and that a good father and husband's role in life was to work hard and be a good provider. The care and feeding of children was a woman's prerogative. And leisure time for family would have to come later, perhaps after retirement.

I left for college long before my father retired. I moved from Boston to the West Coast where I have worked ever since as a bank auditor. My mother died suddenly, right before my father retired. His health started to fail, so my wife and I invited him to move in with us. By that time we had three children. It was good for him to be around the children. I think he was a better grandfather than he was a father. But he died three years after moving in with us. What makes me really sad is that we had just begun to develop a closer relationship.

For some reason, my father's death created a real crisis in my life. I became very distracted and dissatisfied with my own life. It didn't make any sense. My job pays well and offers many perks. It does involve a lot of travel, though. I had vowed to be more available to my three sons than my father was while I was growing up. I made a real effort to be around them and to do things with them. But because of the travel, it wasn't always easy.

At work I would feel guilty about the time away from my family. At home I was distracted by thoughts about the work piling up in my office, and I often slipped back into the office on weekends just to catch up.

Things came to a head after a painful conversation with my oldest son. He hadn't bothered to tell me about an important soccer game in which his team made the final playoffs. I asked him why, and he said, "I just knew you wouldn't be able to make it with your travels and all." I was too stunned to go to work the next day. I felt like a failure in my home life. As hard as I tried to do things different from my father, I had fallen into the same trap. I have to reconsider what it means to be "successful." I only hope it's not too late to recapture some of what I've lost as a parent.

Jim's declared values are the opposite of his father's. But his behaviors aren't. He lives with the tension of equally compelling commitments—to his family and to his work. The result: He has come to a wall where he must face himself as his inner values collide with his outer behaviors. Like millions worldwide, Jim lives with the question of how to fit work and life together in an increasingly complex work world. He is part of an emerging generation of workers where *both* men and women struggle with the same concerns, as the archetypal warrior and healer within battle for the worker's time and attention.

LINKING VALUES TO SUCCESS

Values are our conscious or unconscious beliefs about how the world works or how it ought to. We form our first set of values as children. These are usually the same as your parents or primary caregivers (including teachers and even television, in some cases). Later, as we grow into adulthood, we may challenge and change some of these values, but many remain with us for life. These beliefs feed our inner dialogue and, if we are in alignment, shape our actions as we make decisions and manage relationships. When we choose to do something other than what our strategic outer self says we should, it could be that our values, or our idealized self, has come to the fore.

As Jim's story illustrates, the best way to get an accurate reading of your true values is to look at your behaviors. Most of us talk a good game when it comes to values. But we find it hard to walk our talk. We say we want happiness, but we choose situations that lead to discontent. We say leisure time is important, but we fail to make time for ourselves. We say our health is the most important thing, but we consistently make unhealthy choices. This incongruence is at the heart of much of our dissatisfaction at work. We blame our work when we should take a closer look at self and how we got to a place so out of sync with our values.

Values also determine how we see ourselves and how we want to be seen by others. Do you want to be remembered as engaging and likeable, or do you think it's enough that people respect you and do as you ask? How does your idealized self match up to your social self? A friend says to you, "Wow, you really get off on control, don't you?" You find yourself immediately becoming defensive. You can't stand control freaks. Worse, you can't stand the thought that you might be coming across as one. It could be that you really do value control (hint: most people do), but your idealized value is that you are a flexible, cooperative, caring person who willingly puts the needs of others first.

When was the last time you received someone's feedback and defensively shrugged it off? We tend to do that when it collides with our idealized view of self or when we don't value the opinion of the person giving it. But, if we seek and apply feedback, we become clearer about our lived values (how we behave) and their impact on self and others. If you honestly examine your values, you can sort out those that are *ideals* from those that are *actually lived*, then decide which ones serve you and which ones you'd like to develop or release. You will empower yourself to heal your work, your relationships, and your life.

The process is a spiritual one. It requires making note of your true values, then *committing to think and act accordingly*. For example, if you value integrity or reliability in yourself, then you would consistently keep your word. If you value your creativity, but find yourself in a routine job with few creative outlets, you would make time outside of work to pursue your artistry.

Self-deception is one trap to avoid. When our behaviors are out of sync with what we say we believe in, we tend to use self-talk to delude ourselves into thinking we are really living our values. My clients Bob and Judy, a self-proclaimed workaholic couple, are a prime example. They confessed that each time they missed their daughter's piano recital because of work, they lied to themselves with the following self-talk, "We are working hard to ensure she will have the best of everything in the future."

The fact is, *now* is what matters most. For their daughter "the best of everything" would be having her parents show up. Bob and Judy are practicing to reprogram their self-talk and actions. Their new self-talk is "We are living our values NOW." They are still workaholics and readily embrace their love of intense work as one of their core values. And that's okay. Given this, they have chosen a new behavior to practice that will support them in getting alignment between two competing values: a commitment to work and a commitment to family. They now schedule all of their daughter's activities into their planner as priorities along with their commitments.

Developing a personal definition of success begins with the courage to live from the inside out. As the Quaker proverb goes: "To better hear the world outside, listen faithfully to the voice inside." When work pulls us outside of ourselves into the world of paradoxes and pressures, we must be willing to return again and again inside ourselves to check our internal compass. We must trust that the answers we seek are already within us and we must commit to asking questions of ourselves: What works for you? What makes your heart sing? What just happened, and what lesson is it trying to teach you? Does this choice support your present definition of success?

Consider this story of one man's journey towards a personal definition of success:

JERRY MCNELLIS'S STORY:
"Discovering Myself"

I had polio as a kid. This set up a lot of supposed barriers, but my Dad just saw it as another experiment. "Hmmm. Let's see. How to ride a bicycle with a leg brace." As a research chemist, my father had a very broad tolerance for experimenting. We were never told as children we couldn't do anything we dreamed of. I was encouraged to experiment. So I came up with the idea of hooking my leg brace up to an ice skate. It wasn't very successful, but I had fun.

Later as a Boy Scout, we had to raise $40 for our troop. I'd gotten a hold of a book called *Applied Imagination*, by a man named Osborn. Inspired by his ideas about creative breakthroughs, I came up with one of my own. We had the fifty or so women in our lives knit jersey loop potholders. It cost very little for the raw material, and we sold them throughout our neighborhood. Instead of raising $40, we raised $400, and a business leader was born. By age fourteen I was a leader in the Boy Scout honor society. I discovered that if you make things a great deal of fun, people will stay engaged. When we had to build camp grounds at a local camp, I would suggest we make a contest out of it with crazy prizes. Instead of having hot dogs, I would get the locals to donate different unique kinds of food. We even got local construction firms to bring in bulldozers for free. We kids led the whole thing, directing these grown men.

That's how I came to be doing what I do today. No high school guidance counselor could have pointed me in this direction. Today I help organizations that have strategic issues and need to engage large numbers of people in creative problem-solving. I have been doing this full-time for thirty years. In the early years I worked long hours by myself. The business grew, and I had to add many people, creating complexity and thrusting me into areas I knew little about: cash flow management, technology, hiring, and developing the right people. I had great natural leadership skills, but I lacked the management acumen. The costs were enormous. It was the pits: broken relationships, a failed marriage, and emotional challenges. I had to get help.

I started flying down to Charlotte for counseling from a friend who is a psychologist. I found in him a wise, skilled mentor who I could call at anytime with specific questions. Once when I visited him in a crisis, he simply put me down in front of a large window where I could see the lake, and he put on symphony music and left me there for four hours just to reflect on what I needed in order to be truly alive, truly successful.

When my marriage fell apart in the middle of this, I had to find some anchor points. I turned to my children. That was a good thing, because I had neglected my relationships with them. It was healing. The second anchor point was joining a church. Then I started dating. This energized me and helped me rebuild my shattered self-esteem, which helped me both personally and in my business. I started having fun again. I went from a cocoon to doing things I've never done before. I remember going to a wedding alone. I had always done things as a couple. It never dawned on me I could do such a thing alone. I had so much fun.

Today, the process of healing my life and my work continues. I'm redefining success for myself again. I'm shedding a lot of things, so I can focus on what's important at this stage in my life. For starters, I'm getting rid of stuff. I just took forty cases of books to a used bookstore. I kept only the books that mean a lot to me. I'm letting go of a lot—releasing. I don't know where it's going, but I know it has to do with simplicity, focus, and energy.

I can no longer allow my energy to be diffused. I'm getting ready to leverage my life skills and abilities into something that is still revealing itself. In the meantime, I just keep asking myself, "What is really, really, really important right now?"

Traditional cultural definitions of success tend to be pointed in a single direction: upward. Win as much as you can, exceed expectations, climb the ladder, make the numbers, out produce, out maneuver, outsource to shore up profits. Do it faster, bigger, better than anyone else. I still enjoy succeeding in these ways. It feeds my material hunger and gives me a sense of pride and potency in facing the world and making things happen. No doubt about whether we're running a non-profit social service agency, healing the sick, teaching students, producing goods and services, governing our constituents, or protecting our country, winning—power by achievement—plays a critical role. But winning is not all there is to success.

The trap with this more limited traditional view of success is that it may tempt us to "progress" past where we are happiest on the way to something that may win us accolades but stifles our spirits. This awareness is prompting me to rethink and simplify the mission of my consulting and training practice. With help from a coach, my work is coming into clearer, single-minded focus. I am learning to stop trying to be all things to all people. By stopping the madness of being pulled in multiple directions I hope to become more and more aligned with my singular mission: *to help people find meaning in their work so they attain more satisfying personal and organizational results.* I still consult, write, and lecture, but before making a choice or responding to a client request, I am learning to *stop* and ask: "Will this assignment further my mission or impede it?" "Will it nourish my soul and the souls of those I serve, or will it miss the mark for one or both of us?"

What excites me most is the awareness that a personal definition of success can be liberating and expansive. It does not lock us into an upward trajectory. Because it is neither rigid nor finite it can include our desire to win or excel in the traditional sense, but it can also transcend its narrow confines. Like Tim and Myrna, the couple who chose a life of service in Africa, a personal definition of success changes to accommodate the phases of our lives. It makes room for our individual needs, wants, and interests. It allows room for inaction—to stop and go inward to renew ourselves and our work. It even leaves us the option to spiral downward if we choose to do less in order to be more present for what's important to us. It allows us to fail and to know, as Malcolm Forbes reminds us, "Failure is success if we learn from it."

COMMITMENT FOUR:
SUCCEED ON YOUR TERMS

If we think of values as the rules we live by or aspire to, then success, by definition, is linked to our values. To write our own success story we must, therefore, be intimately aware of the values that are dearest to us—those we would never give up if forced to make a choice.

Action Ideas:

1. List your top fifteen values.

2. Next, review each one and decide whose values these are—Yours? Your company's? Your parents? Did you choose them or were they "imposed" on you? Did they work for you years ago, but not any longer?

3. Next, circle the five values, from among these, that you would never give up if forced to make a choice.

4. Print each of these five on the top of an index card or on separate pages in your journal. Carry these around with you for several weeks. Each time you find yourself in a situation at work where one of these five comes up, or is tested in some way, make a note describing the situation on the card or the page that

corresponds to this value.

5. In a month or so, review all your entries. Explore the following:

- What's become clear, or clearer, to you about your values and how you live them?

- What connections can you make between these values and your personal notions about success?

6. Finally, write your own success story in your journal as though it were an epitaph in which you are looking back on your life and documenting how wonderfully successful you were. Be sure to write it so it exemplifies how you lived each of your top five values.

FOURTEEN

Love The Work You're With

Sitting in the terminal window of Reagan National airport in Washington, D.C., I watch with mild amusement (and, yes, some trepidation) as a slight youngster makes several failed attempts to put a large hose in place to service the plane I'm about to board. The task requires a small ladder, which keeps flipping over. The hose somehow keeps getting trapped under the ladder. The worker dismounts and re-adjusts the ladder several times, obviously cursing out loud. Thankfully, I can't hear the words from where I sit. There is no supervisor or co-worker in sight. I wonder if the plane will get refueled properly. I wonder what it means for someone frustrated to be charged with tasks that can have life or death repercussions. I wonder how this lone worker sees the job and what impact that view will have on all of us.

Safely, and thankfully, I land in the Atlanta airport two hours later. My next encounter of interest is in the least likely of places—the women's rest-room. This worker comes bouncing in for one of many daily rounds of perhaps the most menial job known to man-kind—cleaning the toilets. She is literally whistling as she works. She is wearing a fanny pack that holds a CD player to which she has attached headphones that peep out from under her wide-brimmed rose-colored hat. She whistles as she maneuvers around the cart to pick up after a woman who has carelessly tossed her paper towel on the floor. She whistles and hums, wiping the counters and replenishing the soap. I'm mesmerized. She dances her way into the first stall, and I pause to note whether the whistling stops. It doesn't. I wait for her to re-emerge, approach her, and start to talk. She politely slips the earphones down around her neck to hear me.

"I'm writing a book on work and you've just made my day!" I hear myself gushing. She accepts the compliment, laughing and flings her right hand up to give me a high five. "Yeah girl, I've been doing things this way for fifteen years, and I insist on having a good time. You've got to find a way to love it, or it kills you!" I make a move to return to the high five, but catch myself before my hand connects with her dirty yellow rubber-glove.

I walk away smiling as I recall my meeting with rela-tively privileged managers who spent the day complaining about the hardships of their work life while the toys sat in the middle of their tables. Their concerns were legitimate. But I was struck by the irony of the contrast between the janitor's outlook and that of the managers or of the maintenance employee on the tarmac in D.C. (I don't know what you think, but I'd rather have that janitor fuel my plane.) I am reminded of the power of choice, discussed in the previous chapter, to love the work we're with. We may not be able to choose ideal work conditions, but we can certainly choose to have a more pleasurable experience of our work.

Unfortunately, most workers are so caught up in the day-to-day grind of to-do lists, work orders, performance goals, and earning a paycheck that they lose touch with what is sacred about work. It seems to me that more people focus on the routine aspects of their work—the job—than on the impact on those who benefit from their toil. Rarely is the clerical worker in a hospital aware of how her work connects to patient satisfaction. The reservationist for the airlines does not typically see himself or herself as helping the wheels of the economy keep turning. Even in exalted professions like medicine where the physician gets to save lives, it is easy to forget this connection during a twelve-hour shift spent rushing from the "gall bladder in Room 202" to the "amputee in Room 167."

The sixties song extols us to love the one we're with if we can't be with the one we love. Similarly, making peace with our present work is possible and, in fact, is a necessary step whether our goal is to stay or to ultimately move on.

But this isn't always easy. Anyone who has ever had a difficult relationship with a boss will tell you boss stress is no cakewalk. You dread coming to work. You feel tense and inadequate. Ultimately you can't do your best work. It's no wonder that difficulties with a supervisor is the number one reason people quit. Yet, even in the face of such difficulties, it is possible to find ways to connect with your work in ways that might even contribute to healing a difficult work relationship.

I remember complaining once to a colleague about my boss's leadership style and his difficult personality.

"Have you considered how you might be contributing to the problem?" my colleague asked.

I was outraged. "So now we're blaming the victim," I sulked.

"Well, even if you feel you're a victim, you still have choices," he persisted. "You could quit."

"No, I can't," I snapped. "I owe thousands of dollars in student loans, and besides, I love my students."

"Well, then, perhaps you ought to be grateful you have a good paying job that you basically enjoy. So few people do. Why don't you just suck it up and focus on doing your best work anyway?"

I walked away miffed because instead of lending a compassionate ear, my colleague was unsympathetic and even critical. But he did teach me a lesson about choice I'll never forget. By countering my objections, he forced me to look at my problem from a different angle. It never dawned on me that I had a role to play in how I defined my work experience. I ultimately moved on from that position. But I was able to see my work differently—to feel gratitude for the experience and the pay, and to make peace with my boss and my work before doing so.

Think back to your very first day in a new job. Remember how engaged you were—how you hung on to every word people said? Remember how you politely listened to try to figure out who does what and how intrigued you were by what they did and how it might intersect with what you were hired to do? If you're like me, you worked hard to remember peoples' names and you gave only positive feedback, hoping to win friends and influence people favorably.

In those first days you *chose* to have positive regard for your new situation and the people in it. You *chose* to avoid office gossip. After all, you didn't yet have the lay of the land so everyone got the benefit of the doubt, especially your new manager. Most likely, you *chose*, as the saying goes, an attitude of gratitude for the new opportunity opening before you. You *chose* to love the work you were with at the point of its new beginning.

Now, months or years later, the story may be different for you. Surely, a few of your original expectations are no longer being met. By now you might be a little jaded. You may have hired into healthcare dedicated to a vision of healing humanity. Now you find that managed costs and managed care rule your life. Or, like my friend Marlene who entered the publishing world hoping to express her passion for the written word, you may find your creativity perpetually sapped by office power plays and impossible deadlines.

Perhaps you are among the fortunate. You have the perfect work life in most respects, but find yourself resenting your work because it conflicts with your commitment to family and you are living with the guilt and stress of that reality.

If you are a manager, charged with getting the best out of employees, you may find the earlier euphoria of leadership compromised by a loss of trust on the part of employees as your organization goes through yet another major change. You, like the others, may be wracking your brain and wringing your hands as you face the uncertainties.

As this book has suggested throughout, these are the harsh realities of the work world that, depending on our outlook and choices, can eclipse the joy in our work.

By now you get my drift. We have choices to make in how to approach work. We can't wait for the world to change. We must change ourselves. And we must do so from the inside out. We must choose to look at our work situation with new eyes and see what's good, redeemable, salvageable, and use that to rekindle the love relationship with our work.

COMMITMENT FIVE:
EXPRESS GRATITUDE

It bears repeating—you get to choose how you relate to your work. Making new choices in attitude and orientation requires time and patience. At first, it may even feel hokey. You may have to pretend—in the jargon of psychotherapy—to act "as if" until your true feelings catch up with your behaviors.

What I have discovered, though, is that the surest path to re-igniting the passion in our work is by choosing an attitude of gratitude. So here is a suggested set of practice exercises to try out at work.

ACTION IDEAS:

Practice stopping three times per day—morning, noon, and evening—to express gratitude. You can do this in one of three ways.

1. In your journal, note two or three aspects of your work, or two or three work-related outcomes for which you are truly grateful. It could be something simple like a successful phone call or something significant like closing a major deal. Or it could be some attribute of your position that you particularly like, such as getting out from behind your desk to work in the field some days.

2. Send an email, write a thank you card, call, or visit a colleague or customer to express your thanks for something he or she did, or for simply being.

3. For one minute, brainstorm and list as many things as possible that are positive or that you appreciate about your work. (Keep these lists. Pull them out and read them whenever your morale sags.) This sounds simple, but it's an extremely powerful exercise for re-learning to love the work you're with.

FIFTEEN

Learn to Mix Business With Pleasure

"Work while you work and play while you play..."
So begins a song we sang over and over in grade
school. We learned back then that work is
seriousness business, not to be confused
with play. As a young professional,
the idea got reinforced: "Don't mix
business with pleasure." Again, the
grim reminder: There was work, and
then there was pleasure. I guess that's
what vacations and time off are for. I can
remember as a young professor trying to look,
sound, and act serious, as a committed, mature
worker should.

> "Pleasure in
> the job puts
> perfection in the
> work."
>
> —ARISTOTLE

I quickly crossed the line into intensity and
ultimately into workaholism. There are countless
other sad aphorisms that affirm the dourness of
work. "Another day, another dollar," my pal
Bobby, a blue collar worker who lived next door,
used to sigh as he waved his lunch box at us on
his way to work. At week's end, it was, "Thank
God it's Friday!"

These lamentations are too often accepted as the way we should experience work. "How are things going at work?" I asked a friend recently. "I tell you, I'm having so much fun, I'm almost embarrassed to accept a paycheck!" He was affirming what many people feel—if it's fun, it can't be work.

A week later, I went to deliver a presentation at an off-site conference. The conveners were working really hard at making sure the group of middle and senior managers was having fun. They brought in boxes of Koosh balls, wind-up toys, assorted stickers, crayons, funny hats, and lollipops. The woman who introduced me spent several minutes explaining to the group how they might use the play stuff to have fun. She concluded by saying, "Don't throw the heavier, spiny Koosh balls too hard, or they might put someone's eye out!"

No doubt the spontaneity and levity had gone out of this group long before the lecture on how to have fun safely. Except for a few brave souls who nervously toyed with the gooey stress balls as they asked a question or made a point, hardly anyone touched the toys the whole day. This group is not alone. *Working* at having fun is very much in vogue these days. Often while on the speaker's circuit I meet corporate humor consultants. Most are very good at what they do. They teach employees how to lighten up at work. I have also noticed that fun committees are popping up in many workplaces, taking gag jokes and employee pranks to new lows.

Mixing business with pleasure needn't be hard work. Having fun isn't something we *do*. It's a mindset we bring to work. It's a willingness to take ourselves and our work more lightly. It's an openness to finding enjoyment in the small, mundane places of work.

For years I saw travel as one of the drawbacks of my occupation. I complained about the physical and emotional wear and tear of frequent travel. I complained about the challenge—no, the impossibility—of keeping relationships alive. My constant leaving played havoc with marriage, parenting, friendships, and self-care. To make peace with my work, I had to first accept that this is what I want to do. Then I took it a step further. I learned to reframe travel so it added pleasure to my work.

"Change the way you look at things, and the things you look at change."

—WAYNE DYER

What was once a chore became the pleasure of seeing the world—at my clients' expense. My once lonely hotel room is now a periodic getaway free from the daily chores of housekeeping. My hotel room gives me uninterrupted writing and reflection time. No phone rings there. If my trip is longer than one day, I bring fresh flowers, and incense for my hotel room and create a sacred space for stopping, reflecting, writing, or just being at the end of my workday with clients. In the cities I frequent, I have a support network that includes friends, spas, favorite bookstores, museums, and choice hotels that include exercise rooms and other amenities.

It is not a perfect world. It is my work world, and I have made peace with it. I still arrive at the airport lugging laptop, clothing, bags of books, and training materials. This arduous task now simply means *showing up to serve*. Besides, I delight in people-watching, and what better venue could one ask for than an airport.

REDEFINING YOUR WORK SO IT WORKS FOR YOU

Take a close look at how you spend your day. Where do you expend most of your energy? When you avoid doing the important tasks listed on your to-do list, what are you doing instead? Is what you do instead more fun? More fulfilling? Are the activities that sidetrack you really what you want to be doing after all? Could it be that you are being pulled in another direction because there is a part of you that knows this is what you really want?

I am working on an article and a proposal for a new project simultaneously. Both are buried under the pile of books, papers, bills, and other items on my desk waiting for my immediate attention. So, when I enter my office I do something else: I pick up the latest issue of the *Harvard Business Review* lying on the top of the pile, and read an article or two instead.

Then, before I can tackle the desk, the phone rings. It's an opportunity to visit with my grandchildren whom I haven't seen in a couple of weeks, and I miss them. So, instead of clearing the clutter and paying bills buried under the pile, I go paint ceramics with the grand kids. Returning to the office late at night, I flash back to a poetry class I took a few years ago. The teacher, wanting to impress upon us the importance of being disciplined about our writing offered this insight: "Remember: whatever you work at, becomes your work." With this reminder in mind, I *choose* to be deeply satisfied with both my formal career work and the work that shows up and grabs my attention on any given day. Reading to learn new ideas, playing with my grandchildren, stopping to help a friend in need, pausing to give advice to a young college grad wanting to enter my field—all of this can be fun, soul-nourishing, and very important work.

Again the key is awareness. If we are being pulled helter skelter from one set of activities to another, mindlessly spinning our wheels, we will end up stressed and frustrated. If we practice stopping, we can *choose* to switch gears from the job, to the home, to our hobbies, to a relationship that needs nurturing. We can then successfully engage in all these aspects of being and doing, by giving conscious attention to what feels out of balance, and by knowing when to tip the scales in another direction. As I do the work of writing this book, there are days on end where I must go incommunicado. Relationships get neglected. I am slow to answer email or the phone. I am aware there is a tipping point, though, after which protecting my boundaries degenerates into being plain rude or irresponsible. This, too, must be managed. I must tilt the scales ever so carefully in the opposite direction. I am reminded once again, that a satisfying work life does not come from an absence of difficulties. It comes from the presence of inner peace and enough levity to insist on mixing business with pleasure.

Remember recess time when you were a kid in school? Remember how energizing it was to rush outside, do acrobatics on the jungle gym, race about, jump rope, and then return to class revved up and rearing to go? How about taking a play break for five minutes, every couple of hours at work? Your play break could further your business goals in the spirit of mixing business with pleasure. For example you could log onto *www.Athenaonline.com* and take a five-minute mini course online. At this site you can learn some new interesting business tidbits that might be helpful in your work. Or you could walk briskly around the building a few times, clear your head, get your heart pumping, then return to work.

Several companies (like Nike) actually build a culture of play, exercise, and storytelling into their work culture with great results in work climate and innovation. In fact, as the story goes, co-founder Bill Bowerman developed the famous waffle sole through play as he experimented with pouring rubber into a waffle iron at home. John R. Hoke II, Nike's chief designer, is also big on play as a path to innovation. He sponsors fun design camps that include such playful activities as origami making and musical chairs played in origami-inspired cardboard chairs built by participants. Insights inspired in such games become fodder for design work back on the job.

Like increasing numbers of pleasure-friendly companies, Nike also encourages exercise breaks in the gym on company time, and the payoffs are many. For starters, it creates, a healthier workforce that, incidentally, costs the company less in health benefits. It is also linked to greater creativity and productivity. Yes, the brain does work better when you play. Exercise is also linked to improved outlook and less depression, both of which are sure to boost worker morale in difficult times.

COMMITMENT SIX:
HAVE FUN!

We take ourselves and work too seriously. Just stand on the corner any morning and watch people going to work. They are dead serious as they trod along to the office or plant. Try the same experiment at the entrance to a stadium as the fans roll in for a sports event, and you get the contrast—the laughter and animated conversation in the second case says we're going somewhere fun to do something we really want to do.

The literature on creativity and wellness affirms over and over that play adds a healthy dimension to work. If we learn to infuse our work with play, to have fun and levity and creative sparring at work, we might sometimes say, "Thank God it's Monday!"

ACTION IDEAS:

1. Try making a fun game out of questioning old assumptions about how work works. For example, as I suggested in the invitation that follows chapter six, "The Practice of Stopping," instead of waiting to be sick, why not take a wellness personal day off once in a while—to play when you're feeling perfectly fine?

2. If travel is a part of your work, plan something pleasureable to do instead of whatever your usual routine away from home tends to be. Instead of dining alone in the hotel lobby restaurant, for example, call ahead and invite an old high school or college pal who lives in that city to dine with you or arrange for a facial or manicure followed by a light meal in a fun bistro or bookstore.

3. If you manage others, how about planning theme meetings or bringing in an outside speaker once in a while to lend new fresh perspectives to your meeting?

SIXTEEN

Practice Patience and Compassion

Concern, kindness, patience, consideration, care. Rarely do these words appear in business books. Yet we hope our work leaders extend these qualities to us. We hope as customers that we are treated in these ways. Making peace with our work requires compassion—for ourselves and towards others in the process.

Compassion is one of the core behaviors that leads to trust. To engender trust, we must show competence (evidence that we know what we're doing), integrity (evidence that our word is good), and compassion (evidence that we care—that we have the best interests of another at heart). In our self-absorbed, hectic work lives, it is easy to forget the power of compassion. Things go wrong and we look for who's to blame. Faced with the choice of being *right* versus being *kind* at work, we often choose to be right. But sometimes being right isn't worth the price—broken relationships, low morale, and a loss of trust. Sometimes it is more important to rely on human goodness, to show kindness in the face of adversity.

Luckily we don't have to wait to be in the workplace to begin to practice compassion. There are plenty of opportunities in everyday life. Recently, I drove into the garage late at night at the condominium where I live. Someone was parked in my assigned spot. I was furious. These spots are deeded and paid for by the owner of each unit. My immediate fear-based response was to feel violated—wronged. Some boldfaced person had taken my parking space! "That's it. You will get towed first thing in the morning!" I fumed as I made my way out of the garage and up to the visitors' parking lot for the night.

I went upstairs to my condo, dumped my bags, scribbled a scathing warning note, grabbed a piece of tape, took the elevator back down to the garage, and slammed the note on the windshield. There. Problem-solved: First you warn them, then you tow them. It's over. I didn't sleep well that night. Even though I knew I was right.

The next morning, I revisited the scene of the crime. The specter of the car, still in my spot, relit my fuse. I stormed upstairs to the building manager. "Okay what's the process in this building for my situation? Someone's in my spot!" "Oh, it's simple," he replied nonchalantly. "You just have them towed. We don't get involved, because that's private property. It's your responsibility to just tow them." I went back to the car, this time to get the license number and the make and model in preparation to implement my just solution. I ran into a neighbor whose car was parked next to the trespasser's car. "Do you know whose car this is?" The neighbor shrugged, "Nah. You just have to have them towed. That's all."

Suddenly I felt overwhelmed. I had to catch a flight out of town that afternoon. Out of the blue, I found myself thinking *why don't you wait until you return to take care of this?* That question made no sense, after all I was *right*. My Inner Wisdom persisted: *Remember you have been practicing compassion. Doesn't it apply here too?* I went upstairs, packed my bags, and left for Kansas City.

Four days later I returned at 11:00 p.m. My worst fears were confirmed. The car was still illegally parked in my assigned space. Angrily, I drove back to the visitors' lot. This time, I wondered whether the car was perhaps stolen and abandoned there. I began to doubt my judgment in having waited. It was too late to call a towing company, but I did call the police who ran a check and told me the car was registered to someone who lives in my building. By law, they couldn't divulge the owner's name. *Strange*, I thought. *Something is odd here.* Everyone who lives here knows the rules. I left on an errand the next morning, vowing to call a towing company when I returned home, even though my gut still told me to be patient. Two hours later when I returned home, the car was gone from my parking space. Arriving at my front door, I found a huge gift bag filled with expensive champagne, wine, cheeses, fruit, chocolate, and a note that read: *"We are so terribly sorry that our car has been in your space this week. My husband and I were out of the country celebrating our anniversary. Our son had bor-*

rowed our car while we were gone and parked it by mistake in your space. When we returned from Mexico and went to our parking space we thought our car had been stolen! I know this little gift can't make up for your inconvenience, but please accept it with our apologies."

Clearly my work in this situation was to learn to trust in the goodness of humanity and to practice patience and compassion. My work here also involved trusting my gut— my inner knowing that ultimately said few people would be audacious enough to simply take my space for a whole week, ignoring the posted notes and all. By taking the high road, rather than simply slapping a solution on the seeming problem, I had to live for a while with the polarities of being *right* versus being *kind*, being vindicated versus being forgiving. I learned about the intimate connection between our fears of being wronged by another, and the anger that screams for a swift and punitive resolution. The lesson for me was well worth the effort. I still think about how differently this scenario could have unfolded with the unsuspecting couple returning from a beautiful vacation to find their car impounded, and I feel elevated by my decision to be less rash, less judgmental, and more trusting.

Imagine, then, what it would be like to show up at work, willing to practice patience—to be compassionate as we deal with others, to wait before attacking a colleague's ideas in a staff meeting. Consider the possibilities when we face our fears that our managers might be as fallible as we are, and learn to forgive them for being less than perfect. Picture what it would be like to honor our co-workers by seeing their flaws *and* trusting in their goodness nonetheless. You may discover they, too, become more patient with you.

COMMITMENT SEVEN:
HAVE A HEART

Patience and compassion go hand in hand. Both require a willingness to empathize with another and to believe in human goodness. Both begin with our willingness to first forgive ourselves for being less than perfect, then being open to extending this forgiveness to others.

ACTION IDEAS:

1. Consider a time someone showed you compassion. In your journal describe the circumstance and how it made you feel.

2. Now, recall a time you showed someone compassion. Describe the circumstance and how it made you feel.

3. How might you bring more of this to your work?

SEVENTEEN

The New Bottom Line: Spirit at Work

There is a Zen teaching that goes: "Before Enlightenment, chop wood and carry water. After Enlightenment, chop wood and carry water." What changes about our work after we make peace with it? Nothing. Our work remains the same. We change. Awareness, acceptance, and transcendence ultimately lead to resolution. Like the wise woman whose story follows, we make peace with our work and find meaning in the madness of a somewhat imperfect world.

SUZANNE ANDERSON-ZAHIR'S STORY:
"Spirit at Work"

For years my work was separate from my life. I worked harder and harder but my work wasn't feeding my soul. I was using work to escape from other things. I was, quite frankly, a workaholic.

I have since come to understand that I am Spirit. This understanding has allowed me to unite my life and my work as one. I now understand that my work takes place all the time, whether I'm with family or friends or in the organized workplace. It's simply Spirit calling me to be wherever I am. Wherever I show up is where I'm supposed to be working. I am now connected with Higher Purpose. When we make that connection, there is less need to push. Wherever I show up, Spirit has sent me there for a reason. Whatever clients show up, or whatever situation presents itself, if I am invited to participate in a project or assist a client, I am the one who is supposed to be there for some reason. My work is to figure how best to be in that situation.

Prior to this realization I was scared when a challenging piece of work presented itself. Now I enter curious to see why I was called in to do this work. This was a gradual evolution for me, not a Big Bang. Over time I made a conscious movement away from fear of my own potential.

I have done this through my daily practice of meditation—a simple morning and evening ritual. I breathe fully and enter the void: an empty place where I am unattached to struggle and at one with God. My only desire is to feel my connection with God. I get clear information during this time about where I am supposed to be. I also ask for what I need. I'm not always clear about the specifics, but I find a space to put forth a desire. For example, I ask for clients who appreciate me when I show up, as opposed to specifics about which clients and when.

What I'm looking for is to have my work be in alignment with the spirit, vision, and purpose of my life. This is important because those around me, and my own inner voice, tend to label me as different or weird. In the past this realization fed my fears. So now when I ask for clients that appreciate me I want clients that can engage with my difference, be curious about it in ways that are enlivening for us both.

In making this shift for myself, some of my work is paid work and some of it isn't. I pay attention to balance so that the non-paid work doesn't take over. I enjoy making money. I love the exchange of gifts—what I give and what I receive. I love living well. Even when I give of my services, such as helping my family, I still love an exchange of energy—a hug, appreciation, support, and so forth.

One of the turning points for me was after my father's death. I assisted my father in his transition process. As I helped him at his deathbed complete his life issues, I was initiated into the gift of seeing what happens at the time of transition. Now when people show up in transition I'm called into my work.

This also gave me a clearer understanding of the wall. When I hit a wall it means I have to stop and see what the transition is about. It's a hard place emotionally, but it's also life-giving if you hold the wall, move with it, and get help doing so. But sometimes the wall is a brick wall that says go no further, or it just gets higher until you can't go over it—like in the ending of a relationship or a job.

Suzanne's story reminds us that in its purest form, work is a spiritual dance. Through work we discover our limits and push them, if we choose to. Through work we stretch our minds and expand our capabilities. And, like it or not, over the course of our adult lives our work molds and defines us in powerful ways. As we take on work roles—parent, laborer, manager, craftsperson, teacher, caretaker, politician, healer—our sense of self and our capabilities are defined in meaningful and lasting ways. Of course, work is not the only factor that shapes our identity. But it is a most significant one, especially since work is where we spend the bulk of our waking hours.

When we make peace with our work, we lay our egos down, make friends with our fears, and open ourselves to our humanness. We make choices that support the vision we hold for ourselves and the organizations through which we do our work. We are willing to go the extra mile to serve humanity and achieve winning results for our place of employment. At the same time, we are clear about our values, boundaries, and priorities. We know, for example, that parenting is also important work, and if we fail at it in order to succeed on the job, we're really not that successful after all.

Making peace with work also requires that we become comfortable with paradox. We must learn to dance a figure eight back and forth between the polarities of work. In this dance we must be mindful of the possibility of losing ourselves in the quest for more, vigilant for evidence that our work no longer works, yet remain open to the joys of work and the goodness that resides in humanity and in our hearts.

Most importantly, we must be willing to attend to our inner work. The most significant work we do in preparing to serve others, raise families, and heal our lives is the work on ourselves. Approaching our work from this vantage point is liberating. Whatever we do becomes an adventure in service and soul renewal.

Each worker I interviewed alluded at some point to being pulled inward towards introspection. We stop to attend to our inner knowing and a question poses itself: "If you say your children come first, how come you spend all your spare time at work?" We may shrug it off, but it returns, quietly, persistently calling us to stop, look at our lives, and examine our choices. These inner promptings come as early warning signals. If we persist in ignoring them, they escalate into a full-blown crisis of meaning. If we listen, we can seize the opportunity, over and over again, to journey inward and reconnect with our work as we learn to serve self and others in more meaningful ways.

There is a story told of a traveler who came upon a group of laborers working with bricks in the heat of a merciless summer day. The traveler, noticing how tense and overburdened the workers appeared to be, stopped to greet them. "Hello. What are you doing?" the traveler inquired of the first worker. "Can't you see I'm transporting bricks? Leave me alone; I'm tired," the harried worker retorted.

The traveler approached a second worker who was mindlessly mixing something in a huge container. Again he asked, "What are you doing?" "I'm the mortar man," the second replied, annoyed. "My job is to mix the mortar that will hold the bricks together when they are put in place."

Suddenly, a third worker caught the traveler's attention. Like the first worker, he, too, was preparing to lay bricks.

But unlike the others, he was whistling and singing as he worked. So joyously consumed in his work was this worker, he failed to notice the stranger approaching. Intrigued, the stranger tapped the happy worker on his shoulder, and asked, "And you, Sir, what are *you* doing?" The worker pulled himself up from his back-breaking job, smiled up at the stranger, paused, and pointed to the vast expanse of barren land before them. "Oh," he announced with pride, "I'm helping to build a beautiful cathedral on this site!"

This is one of my favorite allegories. The last bricklayer was having a *pleasurable* experience of work. Why? Unlike his co-workers, he focused on purpose rather than on tasks. By connecting to the deeper meaning in his work—with its ultimate positive impact on humanity—he had transformed a seemingly dull, menial task into what Kahlil Gibran calls "love made visible."

As I complete this book, it is Thanksgiving week in the United States. It's a time to harvest what we have sown and to express our gratitude for the abundance of our planet. It is a time to celebrate family and community and to give thanks for that which sustains us. In the spirit of Thanksgiving, let us remember that work is the Divine flow of energy through us, and between us, as we give and receive, serve and survive together.

Resources

SUGGESTED READING

Ambrose, Delorese, Ed.D. *Healing The Downsized Organization.* New York, N.Y. Random House, Inc., 1996.

_____. *Leadership: The Journey Inward, 3rd Edition.* Dubuque, Iowa: Kendall/Hunt Publishers, 2003.

Bridges, William. *Transitions: Making Sense of Life's Changes.* Reading, MA: Addison-Wesley, 1980.

_____. *Surviving Corporate Transition: Rational Management in a World of Mergers, Layoffs, Start-Ups, Takeovers, Divestitures, Deregulations, and New Technologies.* New York: Doubleday, 1988.

Buckingham, Marcus and Donald O. Clifton, Ph.D. *Now, Discover Your Strengths.* New York: The Free Press, 2001.

Drake, John D. *Downshifting: How To Work Less and Enjoy Life More.* San Francisco: Berrett-Kohler Publishing, Inc., 2000.

Fox, Matthew. *The Reinvention of Work: A New Vision of Livelihood for Our Time.* New York: HarperCollins, 1994.

Hagberg, Janet O. *Real Power: Stages of Personal Power in Organizations, 3rd Edition.* Minneapolis, MN: Winston Press Inc., 2002.

Hakim, Cliff. *We Are All Self-Employed: The New Social Contract for Working in a Changed World.* San Francisco: Berrett-Koehler, 1994.

Helgesen, Sally. *Thriving in 24/7: Six Strategies for Taming the New World of Work.* New York: The Free Press, 2001.

Helliwell, Tanis. *Take Your Soul to Work.* Holbrook, MA: Adams Media Corp., 1999

Honoré, Carl. *In Praise of Slowness: How a Worldwide Movement Is Challenging the Cult of Speed.* New York: Harper-Collins Publishers, Inc., 2004.

Kanter, Rosabeth Moss. *The Change Masters.* New York, NY: Simon & Schuster, 1983.

Kouzes, James M. and Barry Z. Posner. *The Leadership Challenge.* San Francisco, CA: Jossey-Bass Publishers, 1987.

Lazear, Jonathon. *The Man Who Mistook His Job for A Life.* New York: Crown Publishers, 2001.

Kubler-Ross, Elizabeth and M. Warshaw. *Working It Through.* New York: Macmillan, 1969.

McKenna, Elizabeth Perle. *When Work Doesn't Work Anymore.* New York: Dell Publishing, 1997.

Whitney, Diana and Amanda Trosten-Bloom. *The Power of Appreciative Inquiry: A Practical Guide to Positive Change.* San Francisco: Berrett-Koehler Publishers, Inc., 2003.

Whyte, David. *The Heart Aroused: Poetry and the Preservation of the Soul in Corporate America.* New York, N.Y: Doubleday, 1994.

TOOLS

Personal Power Profile. Visit www.personalpowerproducts. com to order this profile based on Janet Hagberg's book *Real Power: Stages of Personal Power in Organizations*, as well as other relevant books and tools.

RETREATS

OseCraft Ventures Unlimited offers transformative retreats led by Suzanne Anderson-Zahir and Kaye Craft. Their typical focus is on deep inner work using music, movement, writing, and other modalities in a spa and/or nature setting designed to promote physical, mental, and spiritual wellness. Call 860-673-0163 or visit www.collaborationsgroup.com/ travel, or www.kcraftassociates.com/travel

International Institute for Transformation whose mission is to assist people to live and work with meaning and purpose, offers retreats and a "Transform Your Work" seminar based on founder, Tanis Helliwell's, best-selling book *Take Your Soul to Work*. Call 403-241-0933 or visit www.iitransform.com.

Omega Institute, Rhinebeck, New York, offers over 300 workshops, retreats, and wellness vacations each year. Call 1-800-944-1001 or visit www.eomega.org.

Index

M

N

O

About the Author

© Andrea London

Dr. Delorese Ambrose is a keynote speaker and consultant to executives and organizations seeking change. She is author of *Leadership: the Journey Inward* and *Healing the Downsized Organization* and lectures internationally as a faculty member of the Institute for Management Studies. An award-winning educator, she also served on the graduate management faculty of Carnegie Mellon University for eighteen years. In 1987, Delorese founded Ambrose Consulting & Training—a firm whose mission is to help people discover the meaning in their work to achieve more satisfying personal and organizational results. She presently resides in Atlanta, GA.

To contact Delorese:
Visit: www.ambroseconsulting.com
Email: Delorese@msn.com
Phone: 404-378-5555